The POWER of a
PENTECOSTAL
RHETORIC

The POWER of a PENTECOSTAL RHETORIC

Dr. Gloria J. Lewis

Tate Publishing & Enterprises

Published by Tate Publishing & Enterprises, LLC
127 E. Trade Center Terrace | Mustang, Oklahoma 73064 USA
1.888.361.9473 | www.tatepublishing.com

Tate Publishing is committed to excellence in the publishing industry. The company reflects the philosophy established by the founders, based on Psalm 68:11,
"The Lord gave the word and great was the company of those who published it."

Book design copyright © 2009 by Tate Publishing, LLC. All rights reserved.
Cover design by Kellie Southerland
Interior design by Tyler Evans

Published in the United States of America

ISBN: 978-1-60696-024-0
1. Religion : Christian Theology : Systematic
09.01.07

Dedicated with gratitude and much love to the one who had the greatest impact on my life and who motivated me to strive for excellence: my mother, Bishop Willie Belle Easley

ACKNOWLEDGMENTS

I am grateful for the assistance of a number of people in the preparation of this work:

Dr. Howard O. Jameson, my counselor and advisor who gave me the confidence that I could complete this study.

My husband, Robert, who made so many sacrifices for the completion of this work.

My mother, Bishop Willie Belle Easley, who always had the utmost confidence in my abilities.

Loretta Henry, my dearest friend, who encouraged and supported me through it all and without whom this work could not have been completed.

My church family at True Holiness Temple who supported me and lifted me up to the Lord in prayer.

TABLE OF CONTENTS

Foreword   11
Introduction   13
The Preacher   17
The Preparation   37
Hermeneutics   55
Homiletics   69
The Presentation   89
Summary   97
Appendix   99

Sermon Outlines
Will the Real Holiness Church Stand Up?   101
Never Saw a Man Quite Like This One   105
For Best Results: Follow Directions   109
God Will Deliver   113

Sermon Transcripts
Amen, Hallelujah   117
Re Me   123
After the Locusts Have Gone   129
The Inner Man Wants Out   137
We Must Go To War   145
What Time Is It?   151

Sample Work Material
Hermeneutics Worksheet   157
Sermon Outline   163
12 Point Alliterative Outline   165
Sermon Plan   167
Checklist of Effective Study Habits   169
Bibliography   179

FOREWORD

Few Christian scholars have so perspicuous a view of rhetoric as does Dr. Gloria J. Lewis. Her life as a preacher/theologian has been tempered at the forge of experience and has given her an unusual insight into the immutable laws of communication success. Her ideas have come from a lifetime of study, preaching, and teaching.

"The Power of a Pentecostal Rhetoric" is not a pedantic manual setting forth easy steps to preaching prowess, nor does it offer any revolutionary methods by which one can hope to become an overnight preaching wonder. What this book does is to present a philosophy of preaching that eschews the extremes of a cold presentation of the Word of God with no spiritual manifestation and a highly emotional presentation with little substance from the Word.

Few authors have ever used more poignant language than that which comprises this text. Its aesthetic appeal, however, is secondary to its intellectual and spiritual stimulation, in that the book seeks as its aim the presentation of a philosophy for balanced, Spirit-anointed preaching. To facilitate that aim, the author mentions some of the most spiritual communication principles known to man.

In reading this book, I am sure that you will find—as I have found—an inexplicable movement within you, which will increase your self-confidence, set definitive goals for yourself, and elicit your positive responses that hold the promise of abundant and gratifying preaching success.

Dr. Howard O. Jameson
Jameson Schools of Ministry and Theology
Philadelphia, Pennsylvania

INTRODUCTION

Many years ago, the Lord Jesus Christ gave a commission to his disciples. He told them to go preach the gospel to every creature. Since then, many men have become disciples and have dedicated their lives to the work of the ministry. Presently, people all over the world are proclaiming the Word of God. While the message is primarily the same, the methodology for its presentation can differ tremendously.

Denominational differences play a large part in the way a minister delivers a sermon. Some preachers strive for excellence in the areas of hermeneutics—the art of correct biblical interpretation; homiletics—the art and science of sermon preparation; and rhetoric—the art of speaking and writing effectively. Others rely solely on the Holy Spirit to give them the message and to tell them how to present it.

The purpose of this study is to identify what may be called a Pentecostal rhetoric, and to consider the impact of the Pentecostal's use of rhetorical skills. Further, in an attempt to discuss its relative effectiveness, the study will differentiate between traditional religious rhetoric and Pentecostal rhetoric.

If the abilities of the minister are to be correctly interpreted, the procedures of rhetorical criticism are necessary. This study will make a critical examination of the Pentecostal minister as a religious speaker, using such rhetorical criteria.

Since the macrocosmic phenomenon of Pentecostal rhetoric will be considered, certain limitations will necessarily be imposed in this investigation. This study will attempt to answer the following research questions:

(1) Is Pentecostal rhetoric different from non-Pentecostal religious rhetoric?

(2) If so, what are the identifiable differences?

(3) What is the worth of the Pentecostal rhetoric? Is it effective?

Contemporary religious rhetoric is highly significant in the world today because of its tremendous impact upon its listeners. There is a concern, however, that ministers are not using this skill effectively because of certain limitations. This study should serve to introduce a remedy for the inefficacious sermon. It should also provide us with an insight into the problems of changing a typical fundamental preacher into one who can successfully penetrate the hearts and minds of the people through effectual delivery of the Word of God.

The interest in this study is in the criticism of the product of rhetoric, that is, the live sermon as delivered. There are many factors, however, affecting any given sermon. Many of the judgments for forces acting upon the sermon lie outside the sermon occasion. A sermon should be viewed as an effect of various causative factors, some of these being in the realm of denominational teachings, some being ministerial training, and others having to do with the specific audience. These factors lie outside specific rhetorical choices of the speaker, yet have obvious influence upon those choices. This study is concerned, in Wichelns' words, with "the analysis of and the appreciation of the orator's method of imparting ideas to his hearers." It is concerned with the faculty of the speaker to discover all the available means of persuasion. Of course, to do this, more than just the sermon must be considered.

As has been stated, when the focus of study is on the "method of imparting ideas," denominational factors, the climate of opinion, the basic assumptions of the speaker, the delivery factors, and the specific audience all must be considered. But the focus of the study is still the effect of the sermon as the speaker presents it. The living sermon is the axis around which all other forces operate. To attempt a description of such a dynamic, interactive situation with mere words is, of course, open to many problems. Denominational factors, ministerial training factors, and even individual opinions become active and interactive forces impinging upon the relationship of speaker-sermon-audience at some particular moment.

Specifically, this study will employ the historical-critical methodological approach to a macrocosmic rhetoric criticism of both traditional religious rhetoric and Pentecostal rhetoric.

THE PREACHER

Not everyone who preaches has received an unction from God. While it is important that the Word is spread around the world, it is more important that the persons who carry the Word have been prepared and sent by God.

In order for the ministry to be effective and successful, the minister should meet certain criteria. These criteria include separation, consecration, dedication, a holy walk, and a total commitment to the work of the ministry.

This chapter will basically cover three particular areas of concentration.

(1) the Call–where we will view the hand of
the Lord moving upon the preacher

(2) the Commission–where we will view the work that the Lord has assigned to the preacher

(3) the Commitment–where we will view the preacher's dedication to the work of the ministry

THE CALL

The call to preach comes directly from God. The manner in which it comes varies from person to person, but it is always divinely inspired. Jeremiah was called by God when he was just a child. Paul, however, was full-grown, well educated and had an established reputation as one who persecuted the church. One might think that these two would be unlikely candidates to carry God's Word, (a child who was frightened and a man who frightened others) but God has never made a bad choice. Human frailties, faults, or failures are insignificant to Almighty God in his choosing of vessels for his use. God is sovereign and can do whatever he wants, when he wants, and with whom he wants. The Lord did not pick names out of a hat at random and decide that they would be the ones to carry his Word. Before the foundation of the world, it was predestinated that specific men would proclaim the Word of God and fulfill his purpose. Warren Wiersbe says:

> God does not call committee meetings; he calls individuals to overcome the world and glorify his name. When he wanted to save a lost world, he called Abraham and founded the Hebrew nation. When he wanted to deliver that nation from bondage, he called Moses. He called Joshua to lead the nation into their inheritance, and Samuel and David to rescue the people when their sins had led them back into slavery. He called Paul to take the gospel to the Gentiles. He called Elisabeth to bear John the Baptist, and Mary to give birth to the Savior. He called Lydia to open up her home for the church at Phillipi, and Priscilla and Aquila to befriend Apollos and Paul.[1]

To be called to preach God's word is a blessed privilege and is to be treated as such. The Lord entrusts his Word to the minister and relies on him to be faithful. This is the greatest call and the greatest privilege to be given to man. The call to be a minister to preach the gospel of reconciliation and to share the riches of his glory is a free gift of God's grace. It is an awesome responsibility that is not to be taken lightly. The minister is called to be a steward (one who manages somebody else's property). He oversees others but remains a servant himself. The first requirement of a good steward is faithfulness. The responsible steward will make God's priorities for his life paramount. He must prioritize the following areas: God (developing a relationship with Him), family (giving loving care and instruction), job (the chosen profession or occupation), and ministry (personal outreach and witness) as well as social activities, hobbies and entertainment. He must also be accountable for the use of time, money, gifts, and the care of the body. God has intentionally planned each person's appearance, voice pattern, abilities, strengths, weaknesses, and other characteristics, as well as his spiritual gifts. It is each person's responsibility to share himself in the body of Christ by demonstrating Christ-like attitudes, and by building up other Christians through the use of his God-given resources.

When the spirit of man becomes aware of the call, it is then his duty to receive it and become available to be used by God. There are many people who hear the voice of God but will not obey. Perhaps they disobey out of fear of what man will say or because of feelings of unworthiness and ineptness for the job. There are many excuses used by man to avoid doing the will of God. However, when God calls man, he accepts no excuses.

Be assured that whatever he tells man to do, he will equip him to do.

Never has the Master Builder employed a carpenter and did not give him the wood, hammer, and nails. Nor has he asked anyone to build for him without first giving him the plan. Furthermore, he has never sent a prophet without a message or an apostle without power. God will not call a person to preach and not anoint, condition, and strengthen him for the work.

God called Jeremiah to be a prophet unto Judah. The following is an account of that call:

> Then the word of the Lord came unto me, saying, before I formed thee in the belly I knew thee; and before thou camest forth out of the womb I sanctified thee and I ordained thee a prophet unto the nations. Then said I, Ah, Lord God! Behold I cannot speak: for I am a child. But the Lord said unto me, Say not I am a child: for thou shalt go to all that I shall send thee, and whatsoever I command thee thou shalt speak. Be not afraid of their faces: for I am with thee to deliver thee, saith the Lord. Then the Lord put forth His hand, and touched my mouth. And the Lord said unto me, Behold, I have put my words in

thy mouth. See I have this day set thee
over the nations and over the kingdoms, to
root out, and to pull down, and to destroy,
and to throw down, to build, and to plant
                                    Jeremiah 1:4–10

The Lord let Jeremiah know that there was no need to
fear because he would be with him. That same assurance is given to all whom God anoints and appoints.

The first call that I remember answering was the
call to righteousness. One night in 1974, I had a very
vivid and disturbing dream. My daughter (who was
five years old at the time) and I were riding bicycles
in the mountains of West Virginia. We stopped along
the mountainside to rest. Shortly after stopping, my
daughter said, "Look, Mommy, there's a man up in the
sky." Naturally, I thought it was her imagination and
tried to discourage her from speaking things that were
not true. Nevertheless, she was persistent and insisted
that I look up because truly there was a man in the sky.
My daughter stood there pointing her finger upward.
Slowly, I looked in the direction that this little finger
was pointing. Expecting not to see anything, to my
surprise I saw the image of a man with outstretched
arms whose hands were seemingly reaching through the
clouds beckoning to me.

A dreadful fear suddenly came over me. The first

thought that came to my mind was, *Oh, God, the Lord has come back, and I'm not ready*. I began to cry and said, "Oh, Lord, if I just had another chance." At that moment, I awoke and realized that it was a dream.

Immediately I heard a voice say to me, *This is your chance*. I knew then that a change must take place in my life.

Shortly after that, one Thursday night, I went to a revival service where my aunt from Fresno, California, was preaching. All that I remember hearing her say that night was, "It's high time to come out of misery and serve the Lord. High time means that it's past time already but you still have a little time left." That night was a turning point in my life. I was called upon to make a decision that would affect the rest of my life. The following Sunday I made the decision to give up the world and follow Jesus. I answered the call. That day I gave the Lord control of my life, and he gave me a deep settled peace. I did not realize at that time that this was the first of many calls that I would have to answer during my lifetime. A few years later, I had to answer another call—the call to preach.

I was born into a family of preachers. My paternal grandfather was a Baptist preacher as was his son (my uncle), both of my mother's parents were Apostolic preachers and six of their ten children including my mother were preachers. While I was proud of my family, it was never an aspiration of mine to follow in their footsteps. I was perfectly satisfied being an usher, a youth leader, and choir director. However, the Lord had other plans for my life.

The Lord came to me in another dream. This time I was preaching. The text was taken from Psalm 107, a scripture that I had never read before. There was also a companion scripture text given, Numbers 14:11. The subject was "O That Men Would Praise the Lord." The message came forth with such power and clarity and the church was tremendously blessed. I woke up and immediately reached for my Bible to find out if the scripture that I had dreamed about was really there. I turned to Psalm 107 and read the words, "O that men would praise the Lord." This was the beginning of events that eventually led me to believe that the Lord was putting his Word in me to proclaim to the world.

Shortly after this, a pastor from a fellowshipping church called and asked if I would come and speak for her congregation one Friday night. She said that she knew that I was not a preacher, but she still would like for me to come and give some words of encouragement. After receiving permission from my pastor, I agreed to go. I prayed concerning what I should say to the people. The Lord had not given me anything else but "O that men would praise the Lord." Therefore, I went to church that night prepared to give the only message that I had.

Our church had fellowshipped with this church for many years. Yet I had never seen the praises of God go forth as powerful as that night. The people were praising the Lord in songs, in the dance, and with testimonies of victory. The glory of the Lord had filled the house and there was a spirit of praise present. I began to panic because I felt that what I had prepared to talk about was inappropriate for that time since everyone was seemingly lost in the praises and God had blessed us so greatly. What could I do? When the pastor invited me to come to the pulpit to speak, I rose with my Bible in hand and slowly walked to the pulpit. By the time I reached the podium, the Lord had spoken to my mind to turn to Numbers 14:11 and the message that came forth through my lips was "How Long Will It Be Ere You Believe?" Oh what an anointing filled the house.

At the end of the service, my mother said to me, "I want you to consider the message that you gave tonight." I then began to seek the Lord concerning his will for my life.

One Thursday night during the youth prayer hour at our church, the spirit of the Lord began to pray through me. I had never experienced an anointing of this magnitude before. Neither had I experienced this type of intercessory prayer before. The Lord had taken complete control of my tongue. The words that came out of my mouth were not my own. After this prayer, I picked up my bible to find a scripture from the Psalms to read at the beginning of the devotion. Instead of the book of Psalms, I found myself in the book of Isaiah, chapter 61. I read the first three verses and then proceeded to turn the pages to get to Psalms. Again, the Scripture to which I had turned was Isaiah chapter 61. This happened three times. I read the passage of Scripture again and finally was able to turn to the book of Psalms. When the service was over, I asked my pastor (who also was my mother) if the Lord would use a Scripture to confirm a work in an individual's life. As she walked away from me she simply stated, "He (the Lord) will make it plain."

I decided that I would research the scripture in Isaiah to find out what it was about. I found that this was a Messianic prophecy concerning the ministry of Jesus Christ. I was so relieved that it was about Jesus and had nothing to do with me. The Spirit of the Lord immediately led me to John 14: 12, which stated, "Verily, verily, I say unto you, he that believeth on me, the works that I do shall he do also; and greater works than these shall he do; because I go unto my Father." By this time, I was becoming very anxious and nervous. I prayed and asked the Lord to give me something more in the Word of God if he was truly calling me to preach. He then led me to Ephesians

4:1, which said, "… walk worthy of the vocation where-with ye are called." I still did not want to accept the fact that the Lord was calling me to ministry.

So I said to Him, "I have always heard that you must wait on your ministry and I don't know when I should go." Immediately, he showed me Ephesians 5:16, which said, "Redeeming the times because the days are evil."

I said, "Yes, Lord," and picked up the phone and called my pastor.

After making arrangements to meet with the pastor, I began to imagine what the meeting would be like. I pictured us talking about the call on my life and after-ward joining hands in prayer and rejoicing. It was going to be a glorious time because I had finally accepted what the Lord had called me to do. Upon arrival at the pastor's home, we had prayer together and the inquisi-tion began. After answering all of the questions posed to me concerning the assurance of my calling, the pas-tor took my hands in hers as she prepared to pray (just as I had pictured beforehand). However, the rejoicing did not come. In its place, I felt heaviness, as if the weight of the world had been placed on my shoulders. If I had not been assured of my calling previous to that moment, I would have thought that I had made a mis-take. I left the meeting in silence wondering what had just happened.

It was not until several months later that I received

the answer. As I was praying one day, the Lord began to minister to my spirit. He spoke to me and said that he had placed the weight of the people on my shoulders but I should not be afraid because he was with me. He would lead me and guide me and uphold me with his power. In the very beginning of my ministry, I was being prepared for leadership.

My life took some unexpected turns. I entered into a vigorous preparation stage to become a spiritual leader for a group of God's people. This leadership would extend from the United States into Africa and Europe.

THE COMMISSION

> Go ye therefore, and teach all nations, baptizing them in the name of the Father, and of the son, and of the Holy Ghost; teaching them to observe all things whatsoever I have commanded you: and, lo, I am with you always, even unto the end of the world. Amen.
> Matthew 28:19–20

The great commission to go to preach was given to the disciples by Jesus Christ after his resurrection and before his ascension. Before this commission could be carried out, there were other requirements to be met. Their understanding of the scriptures had to be opened, and they had to be empowered by the Holy Ghost. The Lord Jesus Himself prescribed the order in which the plan was to be carried out. He told them what to preach and where to begin:

> Then opened he their understanding, that they might understand the scriptures, and said unto them, Thus it is written and thus it behooved Christ to suffer, and to rise from the dead the third day: And that repentance and remission of sins should be preached in his name among all nations, beginning at Jerusalem. And ye are witnesses of these things. And, behold, I send the promise of my Father upon you: but tarry ye in the city of Jerusalem, until ye be endued with power from on high.
>
> Luke 24:45–49

The last commission given to the disciples was to wait for the promise of the Father. This was a promise of power. It was a promise of spiritual equipment for a worldwide campaign against sin.

> But ye shall receive power, after that the Holy Ghost is come upon you: and ye shall be witnesses unto me both in Jerusalem

> and in all Judaea, and in Samaria, and
> unto the uttermost part of the earth.
> Acts 1:8

On the day of Pentecost, this promise was fulfilled. The mighty power of God filled all the house where they were sitting, and they were all filled with the Holy Ghost and began to speak in tongues, as the Spirit gave them utterance (Acts 2:4). What a glorious day! Now the disciples were ready to go forth and carry out the commission. *Preach!*

Immediately Peter began to preach and set forth the plan of salvation. It was done with such power and authority that men were convicted, and the very same day three thousand souls were saved. This power is still present today. God is still moving through his Pentecostal preachers to bring about an inward change in the lives of men. It is the *power* behind the preacher that brings results.

THE COMMITMENT

After man receives power from God, he must learn how to use it. This is accomplished through communicating with the Lord in prayer, and totally committing one's life to the work of the ministry.

Many years ago, my father bought my mother a food processor to make things easier for her in the kitchen.

This appliance included a mixer, blender, and a dicer. In addition, it kneaded bread, along with some other useful features. While my mother appreciated the gift, she continued to do things manually because she had no idea of how to use this "new-fangled gadget." When she wanted to mix batter for a cake, she used a large spoon and mixing bowl. When she needed to chop onions, she used a knife and cutting board. Sometimes when preparing liquid mixtures, she would put the ingredients into a jar, put a top on it, and shake it until it was blended. She manually kneaded the dough for her wonderful homemade rolls while this powerful appliance sat idly on the kitchen counter. She had a clear plastic cover placed over the food processor in order to keep it clean and to display its beauty.

After having all of this "power" on display for a couple of months, she received a card in the mail informing her of free classes available to teach her how to use her newly acquired appliance. She readily responded and learned how to use the power that had been at her fingertips all along but was useless to her because of lack of knowledge.

Power alone is ineffective, but when it is channeled in the right directions, its accomplishments are astronomical. Even though the source of the power is God himself, without a willing vessel, his purpose cannot be fulfilled. It then becomes man's duty to continually yield himself to God, learn his ways, and agree to do whatever he is called upon to do. It is further required that he walk worthy of the vocation with meekness and love with a holy conversation.

Committing one's will into the hands of another will not always be easy. There will be times when the flesh will not want to yield to the Spirit because of fears or lack of understanding as to where the Spirit is leading. However, it is the expression of complete confidence in God when a man will go and not know where he is going, or open his mouth to speak without knowing what he is going to say but allow the Spirit to give the utterance.

Wallace H. Heflin, Jr. writes:

> Every man or woman who is called to preach should recognize that just giving a sermon, any sermon, is not sufficient. God has something specific that he wants to say to his people. We cannot simply repeat the same things over and over. The people we are ministering to today are unique and have unique needs. If God has called us to preach his Word, we have a responsibility to seek his face until we know what specific message to deliver each time we have the opportunity to declare his counsel.

If we are careful to do this, the preaching of the Word of God will never grow stale, or tiring or boring, but will remain ever fresh, ever new, and ever challenging to the people of God. This is his desire.

The anointed and timely preaching of the Word of God can accomplish great things. Through one message from the Word, God can feed everyone present—-from tiny children to the elderly and from the newest believer to the most mature saint And that is nothing short of a miracle. When we are teaching, in a secular sense, the first thing we do is to divide people into groups of similar age and experience.

Then we can teach them on their own level. But God knows how to minister to us all on our own level at the same time— through the anointed preaching of his Word. What a miracle![2]

Regardless of adverse circumstances or conditions, the one called to do a work for the Lord must be steadfast and unmovable, always abounding in the work of the Lord, having the blessed assurance that the work of those who labor for the gospel's sake is not in vain. In addition, man must also make a commitment to learn as much as he possibly can about the Word of God through studying and formal training. One of the greatest qualities that can be found in man is the willingness to learn and grow. In the Apostle Paul's exhortation to Timothy, he said, "Study to shew thyself approved unto God, a workman that needeth not to be ashamed, rightly dividing the word of truth" (II Timothy 2:15). To gain the ability to interpret scripture properly should be a major part of everyone's commitment to further the work of the ministry.

FOOD FOR THOUGHT

- Be sure of your calling.
- Your life should be one of separation, consecration, and dedication.
- God will anoint, condition, and strengthen you for the work of the ministry.
- Ask for guidance in everything that you do.
- Fulfill the commission given to you.
- Tap into the source of power.
- When you acquiesce to the Will of God, it is an expression of complete confidence in his guidance
- Seek God's face until you know what spe-

cific message to deliver each time you have the opportunity to declare his Word.

- One of the greatest qualities that can be found in man is the willingness to learn and grow.

- Be steadfast and unmovable, always abounding in the work of the Lord, knowing that it is not in vain.

THE PREPARATION

Effectiveness in any pursuit largely depends upon preparedness. A general would never lead his troops into battle without an established strategic plan. A building contractor would never begin to erect a structure without an architectural layout. An airline pilot would never leave the airport without a flight plan. On the same premise, a conscientious preacher would never attempt to deliver a message without sufficient preparation.

The process of constructing a message includes the use of good communication skills, a creative mind, and a good understanding of biblical principles. In a sense, the minister is like a general planning to go into battle. He spies out the territory and decides what strategy to use. The preacher can also be compared with an architect who draws a plan for a building. He must decide on a place for everything and put everything in its place. Again, the minister is like an airline pilot who must have a flight plan to know his destination and the route to take in order to reach it.

For thoroughness in planning, the minister must develop an idea through the use of hermeneutics, homiletics, rhetoric, and style. In addition, good study habits are invaluable. These elements will be discussed in this chapter.

THE PREPARATION OF THE MINISTER AND THE PEOPLE

The preacher must not only spend time preparing the message, he must also prepare himself. God's Word is not preached apart from human instrumentality. What the preacher is and what he believes hold a vital place in good sermon preparation. A number of essentials should be taken into consideration.

(1)   The integrity of the speaker–God wants clean vessels. A man's preaching ministry can be made or broken by his personal life and discipline. It is made very clear in the Bible that the minister preaches with his life and his lips. There is a rationale that what a man is becomes more impor-

tant than what he says. Great strength is in the silent sermon of a godly life.

(2)   Convictions about the Word of God–some believe that one's view of the inspiration of scripture is of no significance and not an influence in the matter of preaching. Merrill F. Unger's statement becomes very pertinent:

If the Bible is considered merely to contain the Word of God, rather than actually to be in *toto* the Word of God, there is naturally a decreased sense of responsibility to study its text minutely, or to systematize its theology, or authoritatively declare its message.[3]

---

(3)   The predicament of authority–one's convictions regarding the Word of God will definitely affect one's preaching.

(4)   The devotional life of the minister–as the scientist may possibly lose God in his test tube, the preacher may possibly lose God in his study. He can become so in-

volved in the technicalities of preparing a sermon that he loses sight of the presence of God in his personal life. It behooves the preacher to develop a strong devotional life. Spending time daily in prayer and study of God's Word is paramount in being effective in ministry.

(5)   Prayer–communicating with God through prayer on a daily basis is necessary to effectiveness in ministry.

(6)   Intellectual development of the minister–it is essential that the minister remain a student at all times. He must always be prepared intellectually to the fullest degree of his abilities.

GOOD STUDY HABITS

For a method of planned study to be most effective, particular preparations should first be observed. The appendix contains a checklist for effective study habits. It would be helpful to use it as a guide and for a quick summary of points that will be made in the following paragraphs. You can score yourself on how effective your study time is.

Is your place of study satisfactory? For example, do

you have a place where other people are also studying? You need a place that is relatively free from distractions ... from radio, from talk, from children's activities, and the like. Distractions increase your study time. They increase the amount of energy needed for concentration, and, therefore, make you tire quickly. In general, they just contribute to non-productivity. When ready, start with enthusiasm and don't let anything or anybody distract you.

MAKE STUDYING AN ADVENTURE

Gather all materials needed to collect and record information. Some suggested materials are paper, pens, markers, Bibles (more than one version), dictionaries—including a Bible dictionary, a thesaurus, concordance, and commentaries. Make sure to secure a quiet study area.

During the study process, seven significant steps in the analysis of a passage should be considered.

(1) Express concisely the main points of the text.

(2) Note what is questionable in the passage of Scripture or compare different translations to see if there is any notable disagreement.

(3)   Identify key words or theories found in the text.

(4)   List any historical, literary, or theological issues that are clearly seen in the text.

(5)   Prepare a provisional outline for the passage in keeping with its general context.

(6)   Refer to comparative Bible passages or other related writings where ideas related to the ones found in the text occur.

(7)   Make notes concerning any wider implications the text may contain.

The interest here is in exegesis, not eisegesis. Exegesis means to give an explanation of a Scripture passage. This involves pulling out of the passage what the passage actually says. Eisegesis reads a favored meaning into the passage. An interpretation is exacted upon the passage.

Use your imagination as you read the text. Imagination is very helpful in getting at the truth of the passage. Imagination can take a well-known truth, bring it to life, and give new impressions and excitement. Put yourself into the passage. Imagine you are actually there. Live out what is taking place by role playing the people who appear in the passage. Allow yourself to live what is being taught without letting your imagination run away with you. Be responsible in the way you imagine the text. You will be surprised at how much more resplendent the text will become. It is also helpful to read the passage aloud. Imagine how each speaker would sound and the vocal variety each one might use. Identify yourself with the speaker. The different perceptions such reading will give you is astonishing. Amos Wilder addresses the issue of identification as follows:

> The myriads of men taught by the Bible know that the children of God in his family are all different, and each has his own history, and his own gifts, and his own guilt and his own blessing. Nevertheless our various plots and histories overlap in various wonderful ways, and especially perhaps our moral histories. Therefore we can see ourselves in the stories of Adam, Noah, Abraham, Moses, David, etc.; or in the persons of this or that disciple of Christ or this or that person confronting his death or Resurrection, not to mention Christians of later times or the figures in the Divine Comedy, or Paradise Lost.[4]

When preparing a message or presentation from the Word of God, you should read the text of Scripture no less than five times. Continual reading will give more insight as to what the Scripture is actually saying. A good reference Bible is also helpful in giving other Scriptures to bring even more clarity.

Additional things needed for study to be fruitful include a set time allotted for study, an attitude of prayer, and an open mind. If you study on a consistent basis, you will always be ready when called upon to expound the Word. The Lord will give you what to say at the needed time. Do not move out on the premise of "If I open my mouth, He'll speak for me." If you have not studied, when you open your mouth all that will come out will be hot air.

We would be wise to take the advice of the Apostle Paul to Timothy when he wrote:

> Study to shew thyself approved unto God,
> a workman that needeth not to be ashamed,
> rightly dividing the Word of Truth.
> II Timothy 2:15 (KJV)

DEVELOPING THE IDEA

The expositor must be aware of the central theme of the sermon as well as the type of audience who will receive the message. He should define the purpose of the sermon to be delivered as a message of encouragement, deliverance, comfort, etc. He should identify the occasion for the message, and he must be careful to avoid ideas that would be inappropriate for the audience. For instance, the preaching of a funeral message at a baptismal service would be the height of impropriety. Accordingly, many variables must be taken into account before the final message is fully developed.

After considering the occasion and purpose of the sermon, the preacher must decide the methodology to employ in developing it. Many of my ideas come from everyday living. Something may happen to me during the course of the day and a word or a phrase will come to mind. Often it is pertinent to the idea that I am formulating. God is always trying to talk to us to give us aid in our development of ideas for our sermons. He is always in the "know" regarding when our next sermon will be preached and to whom it will be preached. We should always try to keep in touch with the Master and be available and open to his ideas. I love to receive illumination from God. Such enlightenment lets me know that he is concerned about my organization and delivery of his Word to his people.

Most people have heard the scripture preached many times where God told Moses that if he opened his mouth, he would speak for him. Many take this to mean that opening their mouths is all that is necessary for effective preaching. This indubitably is not the case. The individual who is full of zeal, with little or no knowledge, and has not studied, may open his mouth, and be left with a huge foot therein.

There must be a period of time spent in developing the ideas that God gives us. We have to study and research those God-given ideas. When we have given our all to the preparation of the sermon, God will step in and give his approval. That steward who has diligently prepared himself to feed the flock of God can be confident in his presentation.

Developing the sermon entails the setting forth of one's ideas in clear concise language that will make visible the unfolding mysteries of the kingdom of God. A sermon that is God-inspired and properly developed holds the potential to enable the congregation to attend their senses in decoding the message. Metaphorically, they will be able to feel, touch, taste, see, and hear what thus saith the Lord. Any message that fails to accomplish this has not been properly developed.

FORMULATING THOUGHT

The thought process is of vital importance in the developing of a sermon. However, thoughts without form are useless. Your thoughts must take on form before they can be effective, as a naked body needs clothes before appearing in public. Unorganized thoughts presented in a sermon will only foster confusion. It is like one setting out on a journey but has no idea of how to reach his destination.

When an artist wants to produce a masterpiece, he starts with an idea first. The idea begins to take on form during the sketching stage, but the image is not painted on canvas until the form is completed. Even if the artist has more than one work in the making at the same time, he devotes enough time to each to make sure they are perfect before showing them.

Each sermon should be viewed as a work of perfection. It should not be presented until it is complete in every part. Let us look at some ways to bring form to thoughts.

(1) Research the idea (thought) to make sure that it is biblically sound

(2) Gather related material

(3) Find accounts of Scripture that express the idea

(4) Use pertinent examples

(5) Compare historical accounts of Scripture with today's contemporary audience

(6)   Connect similar thoughts

(7)   Make a smooth transition from one point to another

The average person's thought pattern is not one of concise order. There is such a thing as "confusion of thought." You might start out with one particular thought, and as it expands, you gain more and more information surrounding it. After so much information is gathered, you might begin to wonder what the original idea was. Therefore, it is important that you bring order to your thoughts. Take time to outline your information, placing related materials in groups under the appropriate headings.

If a preacher were to give an account of the death, burial, and resurrection of our Lord and Savior, Jesus Christ, he would not start with the women going to the tomb with spices and then proceed to Calvary the place of death. Death must precede burial and resurrection. Avoid mixing events in a disorderly fashion. This will only tend to confuse the audience and make it difficult for them to follow your train of thought. Order in a presentation will maintain the audience's attention and will keep them anticipating the next thing to come. You must gain the attention of your audience in the beginning of your discourse and maintain it until the end.

Fred B. Craddock lists various forms that "have demonstrated repeatedly that they can carry the burden of truth with clarity, thoroughness, and interest, and, therefore, have come to be regarded as standard":

- What is it? What is it worth? How does one get it?
- Explore, explain, apply
- The problem, the solution
- What it is not, what it is
- Either/or
- Both/and
- Promise/fulfillment
- Ambiguity, clarity
- Major premise, minor premise, conclusion
- Not this, nor this, nor this, nor this, but this
- The flashback (from present to past to present)
- From the lesser, to the greater.

Since most of these forms are found in the Bible, chances are that one of them is particularly suited for the selected preaching-text. If not, another form may need to be devised, for the object is to present the sermon in a form that will do justice to the text as well as to the purpose and theme of the sermon.

Whatever form is chosen, all sermons ought to aim at the clarity, pointedness, and coherence of the didactic form and the vividness, movement, and total listener involvement of the narrative form. In practice, this requirement means that within the overall form of the sermon preachers may wish to incorporate other forms: narrative portions in a didactic sermon and discreet teaching in a narrative sermon. For no matter what form is used the sermon ought to address the whole person; the sermon ought to be life-size in the sense of touching all the keys on the board rather than only intellectual or emotional or volitional.[5]

Keeping an open line of communication with God is indeed particularly meaningful. Communication is defined as the process of sending and receiving symbolic cues whether verbal or non-verbal. The communication process is rather complex. Each individual has his own attitude set. This includes the individual's total of all beliefs, values, opinions, attitudes, and expectations. All of our interpretations are formed on the basis of these sensibilities and past experiences. In fact, even the way in which we learn to interpret things today will have an affect on the way we see things in the future. Because of man's attitude set, he sometimes does not hear the Word of the Lord the way that it was purposed to be heard. He comes to his own conclusions instead of seeking an understanding from the Lord. The Lord directs all who acknowledges him and keep their ears open to really hear him speak.

THE TONE

Another area of consideration should be the tone of the message. The manner in which a Scripture text is expressed is of utmost importance. In some instances, it may be wise to adopt a conciliatory tone. At other times, it may be necessary to use an authoritative manner. The minister should set the tone of the message in the beginning stages of preparation so that when the sermon is delivered it will have an impressive rhetorical effect.

The type of sermon that will be delivered has a great impact on the tone of the discourse. Let's take a look at some kinds of sermons:

(1) Topical Sermon—one that is built around a particular subject or idea. The minister usually gathers what the Bible teaches about a particular topic, and organizes the scripture passages into a logical presentation.

(2) Textual Sermon—is one based on one or two verses of scripture. The main theme and the major divisions of the sermon are derived from the text itself. This ser-

mon seeks to explain what the text itself actually says.

(3)   Ethical Sermon–is taken from a specific passage of scripture that directs an ethical message to the believer. The purpose of the sermon is to build biblical morality into the lives of the people attending worship.

(4)   Allegorical Sermon–this type of sermon takes specific bible narratives and gives them an allegorical interpretation.

(5)   Biographical Sermon–presents a study of the life of a particular Bible character. The facts about the character form the basis for a message with modern applications to appeal to today's society.

(6)   Dramatic Monologue–In this type of sermon the minister becomes the character he is striving to present. He acts out the message of the character in the pulpit. Authentic Bible attire is sometimes used for emphasis.

(7)   Expository Sermon–one that expounds

a scripture passage, organizes it around a dominant theme and major points, and then decisively applies its meaning to the listeners. Choose the sermon, set the tone, and prayerfully prepare the presentation.

The power of Pentecostal rhetoric is very unique, because that power to influence, control, and rule can be with adulation and construction or it can be abusive and destructive. Keeping in mind who our Maker is and who we are representing is of paramount importance. We must never lose site of our mission to spread the gospel to every creature in a manner that is understandable and acceptable. In the following pages, we will take a look at some prerequisites to good sermon preparation.

HERMENEUTICS

An important factor in developing a sermon is the use of hermeneutics. One must have the right attitude and approach to the scriptures and should work diligently to understand them. Hermes was the god of art, science, literature, and speech. Hermeneutics is defined as the study of the methodological principles of interpretation. Jerry Vines says, "Hermeneutics may be defined as the science of expounding or interpreting what a passage of scripture says."[6] The use of science and art are employed in hermeneutics. Science meaning systematized knowledge or rules, and art meaning skill acquired by study, experience, or observation. I contend that a simple explanation of hermeneutics is the art and science of correct biblical interpretation. We need to apply the use of hermeneutics basically for two main reasons: one, to find out what God said, and two, to find out what it means.

The fundamental presupposition about the Bible that sets apart believers from unbelievers is that the Bible is God's revelation of himself and of his will for man's life. Although Christians are united in that fundamental declaration, the implicit understanding of the statement is viewed in very different ways. It is important to understand those different views, for a person's presuppositions will largely determine how he understands and interprets Scripture. Ernest Best explains it in this manner:

> We must know ourselves … Each of us approaches Scripture with his own, or her own presuppositions. These presuppositions are part of our world view, part of our personal theology. In the first instance they relate to the way we regard Scripture. Does it consist of infallible propositions? Is it the record of certain acts of God? Is it an inspired record? Is there revelation outside Scripture? Our views here will dictate how we handle the text. Our minds are not empty when we read or listen to Scripture; what we hear is already partly predetermined by what is

already in them; our presuppositions shape
what we understand. It is not necessary
to argue here for any one particular set of
presuppositions, but to insist that we become aware of our own so that when we
understand and interpret we know how
we are being influenced by them. It is also
important that we see that our presuppositions are consistent, that we do not operate
with one set at one time and with another
at another.[7]

While all Christians believe that the Bible is the Word of
God and reveals the will of God to man, not all Christians
interpret the scriptures in the same way. For example, the
apostle Paul said to Timothy, "Drink no longer water, but
use a little wine for thy stomach's sake and thine often
infirmities" (I Timothy 5:23). Several interpretations of
this verse have been offered. One contends that since Paul
told Timothy to drink wine, it's all right for all Christians
to drink wine. Another avers that there is nothing wrong
with drinking wine as long as it is for medicinal use and as
long as you don't get drunk. Still another states that unlike
today's wine, the wine in Paul's day contained no alcohol
and, therefore, could not have caused Timothy to become
inebriated.

Are any of the above interpretations correct? More

importantly, what is the correct methodology to interpret scripture so that one can tell what the scripture really means? If the Word of God is to be interpreted correctly, it must be interpreted literally. That is the method by which each word is given the same basic meaning it would have in normal, ordinary, customary usage. Any other method of interpretation will result in distorting the truth, veiling the true will of God, and leading one astray.

The following principles of literal interpretation should be employed in our exegesis of the scripture:

(1) Interpret each word separately.

(2) Interpret words within the context in which those words appear.

(3) Interpret in view of the immediate historical setting.

(4) Interpret the grammar of the original language in which the passage was written.

In addition, there must be a distinction made between literal and figurative language. This is done by using the following rule: If the literal meaning of any word or phrase makes good sense, it is literal. But, if the literal meaning does not make sense, it is figurative.

Interpretation of Scripture must also include a look at background setting; who is speaking; to whom are they speaking; background of the speaker; the occasion, historical and cultural setting, word usage in view of the original language; tense—past, present or future.

TYPES AND SYMBOLS

The word *type* is related to the Greek word *typos*. The basic ideas associated with the word *typos* and its corresponding synonyms are the ideas of likeness, resemblance, and similarity. A type can be defined as a person, event, or institution that prefigures something to be fulfilled at a later time. The type is found in the Old Testament and the fulfillment (antitype) is found in the New Testament.

Some examples of types:

Type	Type Of
Adam (Person)	Christ as the head of a race
Moses the Prophet (Office)	Christ
Sacrifices (Institution)	The Cross
Lifting up the brazen serpent (Action)	Crucifixion
Tabernacle (Thing)	Incarnation

A symbol is used to stand for something and is usually the same thing all of the time.

Examples of symbols:

Symbols	Stands For
Leaven (thing)	Sin
Seven (number)	Completeness
Purple (color)	Royalty
Lion (animal)	Ruler/Power

THE PROBLEM OF HERMENEUTICS

The problem of hermeneutics is relating texts that were written thousands of years ago to the present society in the twenty-first century. The more specifically significant a biblical principle was for its own time, place, and circumstances, the less specifically significant it is likely to be for our time, place, and circumstances. However, one cannot ignore the literary, cultural, and theological context of the scripture text. Many interpreters have resorted to the use of analogical, typological, and allegorical methods of biblical interpretation. Augustine and Origen, who were early church fathers, used the allegorical method to relate the text to their times. Allegorism is the method of interpretation that regards the literal sense as the means for a secondary more spiritual and more philosophical sense. The allegorical method does not interpret scripture. The basic authority is the mind of the interpreter and not the scripture itself. Allegory was created when Philo tried to make Old Testament Scriptures compatible with Greek philosophy.

Different cultures or ethnic groups, religions, and denominations tend to interpret Scripture according to their specific needs or beliefs. Jews do not view Scripture in the same manner as African Americans. Pentecostals and Methodists have a different approach, as well as Catholics and Jehovah's Witnesses. The list of differences goes on and on. So then the task at hand is to put aside cultural and denominational differences and find a common bond.

The duty of the interpreter is to find the intended meaning of the author of the text. Therefore, it is imperative that a concise exegesis of scripture is employed. An in-depth investigation of the text should be made in order to ensure proper usage and application of the principles of the scripture. Eisegesis, on the other hand, should be avoided. That is, reading into the text what one wants it to mean. Many ministers have erred in this area by not diligently researching Scripture.

IMAGINATION IN INTERPRETATION

There is some controversy surrounding the use of imagination in interpretation of scripture. However, when it is used properly it can propel one into scripture and incite a deeper understanding. Scripture is more than a body of theoretical thought and inferences. It is usually very concrete, especially in delivery of the sequence of events. In these narratives can be found a myriad of images and the use of symbolic language. These are not always grasped with the intellect alone but also with the imagination.

Joseph Johnson, Jr., a black biblical scholar and a bishop in the Christian Methodist Church, recorded some principles of interpretation to suggest a way of preparation for the imaginative use of Scripture:

1. Prepare yourself with devotion and prayer prior to your encounter with the Scriptures.

2. Read the entire chapter in which the text is located.

3. Become acquainted with all of the stories which lead up to the text and those that follow.

4. What were the problems, the situation of the participants in the story?

5. Read the biblical passages aloud, so as to hear the Scriptures and permit them to speak to you.

6. Discover the human element and the Divine element in the situation.

7. You must see what the writer saw, feel what the participants in the story felt, and hear what they heard.

8. Use your imagination and put yourself in

the place of the writer and participants of the story.

9. Assume the different roles of the principal characters in the story and act as if you were present when the story was first told.

10. Ask yourself this question, "What special message does this passage of Scripture bring to your people for their healing and renewal?"

11. Then wait for God to speak.[8]

When using the imagination in interpretation, you must be very careful not to allow the imagination to overpower the historical facts. While deepening our understanding and bringing more excitement and incite through imagery, we do not want to lose site of the intended meaning and basic principles.

WHAT'S IT ALL ABOUT?

Henry A. Virkler, in *Hermeneutics Principles and Processes of Biblical Interpretation* sums it all up in this manner:

Hermeneutics is the science and art of biblical interpretation. General hermeneutics is the study of those rules that govern interpretation of the entire biblical text. Special hermeneutics is the study of those rules which govern the interpretation of specific literary forms, such as parables, types, and prophecy.

Hermeneutics (applied exegesis) plays an integral role in the process of theological study. The study of canonicity attempts to determine which books bear the stamp of divine inspiration and which do not. Textual criticism attempts to ascertain the original wording of a text. Historical criticism studies the contemporaneous circumstances surrounding the composition of a particular book.

Exegesis is an application of the principles of hermeneutics to understand the author's intended meaning. Biblical theology organizes those meanings in a historical manner while systematic theology arranges those meanings in a logical fashion.

Hermeneutics is essentially a codification of those processes we normally use at an unconscious level to understand the intended meaning of another person. It is only when something blocks our spontaneous understanding of another person's message that we recognize the need for some method of understanding what they intended. Blocks to spontaneous understanding of another person's communication arise when there are differences in history, culture, language, or philosophy between ourselves and the speaker.

There are several issues that affect how one will "do" hermeneutics. We must decide whether Scripture represents the religious theorizing of the ancient Hebrews, divinely-guided and infallible writings written by men but initiated and superintended by God.

We must also decide whether there is a single valid meaning of a text, or whether any individual application of a text represents a valid meaning. Other issues that affect how we will do hermeneutics include (1) whether or not we believe that God's intended meaning includes a fuller sense than the human author's, (2) how to determine when a passage is to be interpreted literally, when figuratively, and when symbolically, and (3) how one's spiritual commitment affects one's ability to understand spiritual truth.[9]

HOMILETICS

While homiletics can formally be defined as the art and science of sermon preparation, homiletics simply stated, is the *modus operandi* of preaching. Andrew Blackwood states that, "Homiletics is the science of which preaching is the art and the sermon is the finished product."[10]

It is not enough just to have a good subject or a good idea for a sermon. The development of the sermon should be based on an understanding of the scripture text and a practical application of the same. In order for the message to be effective, the minister must be able to give an explanation or critical interpretation of the text. He then becomes an exegete.

I once heard a sermon that may have been entitled, "God Will Deliver." The preacher concentrated on the three Hebrew children in the fiery furnace. The story was told about how Shadrach, Meshach, and Abednego would not obey the king's decree to bow down and worship the golden image he had erected. The speaker's main emphasis was placed on Daniel 3:17 which states, "If it be so, our God whom we serve is able to deliver us from the burning fiery furnace, and he will deliver us out of thine hands, O King." After what seemed to me an excessive amount of stomping, yelling, and clapping of the hands, the preacher ended the sermon by relating that the Hebrew children were delivered unharmed from the fiery furnace. While this story was true and wonderful, one was forced to wonder how it related to the contemporary listening congregation. What should have been a message of encouragement somehow became a bible story with much emotion but with no application.

This same scripture text (Daniel 3) and subject (God Will Deliver) can be developed into an encouraging and edifying sermon (See Appendix D). The sermons preached to today's congregations should be applicable to present-day conditions and circumstances. It is good to know that God delivered in times past, but it is better to know that he still delivers people today.

In order to properly prepare a biblical discourse, you must first understand what preaching is. T. Harwood Pattison defines preaching as "the spoken communication of divine truth with a view to persuasion." It covers three points: its matter, which is divine truth and tells us what to preach; its manner, which is divine truth spoken and tells us how to preach; and its purpose, which is divine, truth spoken with a view to persuasion and this tells us why we preach. The preacher must be totally concerned with the delivery of the message from the mind of God to the heart of man. The pulpit is not a place for speculation, venting personal frustrations, expressing political viewpoints, or putting flesh on parade for personal ambitions. The most effective preaching will consists of words about the Lord and words from the Lord. If the preacher's ideas and opinions do not line up with the word of God, they do not amount to a hill of beans in a forty-acre field.

Learning the art of sermon preparation and preaching should be the goal of every God-called minister who is sincere about his vocation.

THE TEXT

The text is most commonly defined as the words of scripture read by the preacher from which he proposes to speak. Most often, the text is detached from the context. It is not necessary for the text to call for a discussion of the context; however, it must be used as to do no violence to the context. The structure of the text should be such as to show respect for rhetoric and more importantly respect for the Bible. Scripture verses should not be butchered for the sake of obtaining a spectacular or impressive text. The text should form a complete sentence. However, if properly used, fractional texts can be impressive. "Reconciled to God" and "Unsearchable Riches" represent a lawful use of Scripture fragments.

The text must be treated reverently and intelligently:

(1) There is no good reason for intentional misuse of a text

(2) Make sure that your motives are right

(3) Be cautious of deceptive texts

(4) Careful study should be given to thwart ignorance

(5) Do not spiritualize texts that have a natural meaning

The text should also be appropriate for the theme:

(1) The integrity of the subject should decide the choice of the text

(2) The preacher should be conscientious in the choice of texts

(3)   The text should suggests the theme

(4)   The text should also distinctly declare
       the theme

The length of the text should be determined by the theme. Short texts often stifle attention, while a longer text brings with it the impression of completeness and power. It is advisable that the preacher occasionally take his text from more than one Scripture passage. It is a useful tool to have corroborating texts. It tends to bring credence to what is being said.

DESIGNING

The development of the ideas of the sermon always should manifest an element of creativity. In particular, sermon preparation should employ deliberate purposive planning. The manner in which a religious discourse is developed has a great bearing on the impact of its presentation. Henry G. Davis gives the following rendering:

Design for a Sermon

A sermon should be like a tree.

It should be a living organism:

With one sturdy thought like a single stem

With natural limbs reaching up into the light.

It should have deep roots:

As much unseen as above the surface

Roots spreading as widely as its branches spread

Roots deep underground

In the soil of life's struggle

In the subsoil of the eternal Word.

It should show nothing but its own unfolding parts:

Branches that thrust out by the force of its inner life

Sentences like leaves native to this very spray

True to the species

Not taken from alien growths

Illustrations like blossoms opening from

Inside these very twigs

Not brightly colored kites

Pulled from the wind of somebody else's thought

Entangled in these branches.

It should bear flowers and fruit at the

Same time like the orange:

Having something for food

For immediate nourishment

Having something for delight

For present beauty and fragrance

For the joy of hope

For the harvest of a distant day.

To be all this it must grow in a warm climate:

In loam enriched by death

In love like the all-seeing and all-cherishing sun

In trust like the sleep-sheltering night

In pity like the rain.

(This is not an attempt at a poem. It is the design of an idea (the first line) and of its development. It is the sketch—the notes, the outline—of a lecture delivered more than once. The lecture is longer than this. But it does not say more than this or does it say it better than this—perhaps not so well.)

OUTLINING

Rousseau, describing the unorganized love letter of a young man to his girlfriend, said, "He had begun without knowing what he was going to say, and he finished without knowing what he had uttered." The absence of a clear logical sermon outline will not allow the preacher to communicate the central theme in an orderly manner. Herbert Spencer said, "When a man's knowledge is not in order, the more of it he has, the greater will be his confusion of thought."

One of the advantages of a sermon outline is that it enables the preacher to bring structure to his message. It discourages thought wanderings and keeps the preacher on course throughout the presentation. The outline should be logical and easy to remember. If alliteration is used it should be done properly, making sure that all alliterative points are: the same parts of speech; beginning with the same letter or syllable or ending with the same syllable and taken from the text itself. Alliteration is the successive use or frequent recurrence of the same initial letter or sound at the beginning of two or more words. Example:

In a sermon on St. John 3

The Must of the New Birth
The Mystery of the New Birth
The Means of the New Birth

Note that all three words (must, mystery, and means) begin with the same letter and are all nouns. Further illustration of an alliterative outline can be found in the Appendix.

RHETORIC

The art of speaking or writing effectively is called rhetoric. This skill is used in all types of communication. Anyone who will be addressing an audience should acquire and develop a mode of language or speech to ensure effectual verbal communication. A master of rhetoric exudes an air of eloquence. Ralph Waldo Emerson defined eloquence as "The art of speaking what you mean and are." At another time he added, "The reason why anyone refuses his assent to your opinion, or his aid to your benevolent design is in you. He refuses to accept you as a bringer of truth because, though you think you have it, he feels that you have not. You have not given him the authentic sign." These words suggest the idea that when a speaker is establishing credence in his own character, he is at the same time inclining the minds of his hearers to readily accept his message.

According to Thonssen, Baird, and Braden,

Aristotle observed that a speech was composed, or grew out of the interaction, of three elements: the speaker, the subject, and the persons addressed. He added that of the three elements, it was the last, the audience, that determined a speech's end or object ... for the speaker, the audience is the most important element in the situation, and that, if he is to be effective, the speaker must adjust both himself and his ideas to it.[11]

Delivering a sermon is like making a speech only on a spiritual level. The congregation then becomes the focal point and the speech should minister to their needs. The audience or congregation takes three things into consideration in evaluating the worth of a speech or sermon:

(1) *Pathos*–the ideas, beliefs, and attitudes in the audience when they come

(2) *Logos*–the actual speech or sermon itself

(3) *Ethos*–what the audience thinks the speaker is

The most important element here is *ethos* because the audience's opinion of the speaker determines how well the presentation is received.

STYLE

Style plays an important part in the delivery of a sermon. A minister can benefit from understanding the three levels of style as proffered by Aristotle, among other ancient teachers. The plain, or low style, is characterized as that style a speaker uses to communicate factual information. This style is undecorated and emotionless. When the speaker desires to impress or persuade, however, he moves to the middle style. Although, as in the plain style, the content is factual and logical, the middle style presents it in such a way that warrants the listener's attention. This level of style is marked by vivid and energetic actions and an appropriate use of the figures of speech. The high style displays an abundance of embellishment. In some hands, this style became grandiloquent or overblown; to ears in modern times, it sounds a bit overdone.

All three styles may be used effectively in one sermon. William H. Kooienga states this about the three styles.

> Some speakers err, however, when they fail
> to think through their use of style and em-
> ploy one or more of these levels inappro-
> priately: what ought to be an urgent plea
> is stated in the matter-of-fact, plain style,
> while material that should be taught in a

clear, controlled manner is delivered as if to
warn people of a fire next door.[12]

David Buttrick expresses style and preaching in this
manner:

> Can you imagine Jesus commissioning dis-
> ciples by saying, "Go into the world and
> fulfill yourselves?" Not easily! The scrip-
> tures are not wild about self-fulfillment.
> Instead, we are advised to lop off an offend-
> ing arm should it get in the way of neigh-
> bor love. Likewise, we cannot conceive of
> Jesus advising preachers to step into pul-
> pits and "Develop your *own* style!" Style in
> preaching is not something we possess in
> order to express our own uniqueness; style
> is neighbor love in language. So we will not
> strive to have a style, but rather we will use
> styles for the preaching of the gospel and
> the forming of faith.

> The preoccupation with developing our own
> distinctive style in the pulpit is strangely
> adolescent—a preoccupation with identity.
> It is almost better to bypass the category
> of style altogether and, instead, think of

how we can speak so as to match words with content, with point-of-view, and with intentional purpose. Oddly enough, as we develop linguistic range, as a byproduct we may find our style given!

Appropriate style is a key to effective speaking.

DEMONSTRATING

The use of demonstrations in a sermon can add color and excitement. However, it is imperative that the speaker uses discretion in his choice of demonstrations so that he will not alienate his listening audience. For example, one would not use visual aids when speaking to a group whose vision is impaired. Again, one should make sure that whatever demonstrations used fit the occasion and are in good taste.

At the beginning of the year, I was the evangelist in an evangelistic crusade held in a local church. The Lord had given me the theme "Prepare for the Rain." The first night of the crusade, I instructed the ushers to distribute tiny decorative umbrellas to everyone in the congregation. The members of the congregation were then told that throughout the crusade these umbrellas would serve as a symbol to remind them of the showers of blessings the Lord had in store for them. They were to hold their umbrellas upside down to catch the blessings. This was the first time I had used a visual aid of this sort but the results were remarkable. The people faithfully brought their umbrellas to service every night of the crusade with expectations of receiving showers of blessings from the Lord. They were not disappointed. The Lord rained down blessings from on High and satisfied many thirsty souls.

The minister can explore many different avenues of demonstration. The more creative one becomes, the more enlightened the audience. Many times, mere body language (i.e. hand gestures, facial expressions, etc) is sufficient in expressing an idea. At other times, one might use short illustrations related to the subject to reinforce a particular point. These illustrations may include personal experiences, accounts from Scripture texts, antitheses, or short stories. Imagery can also be used within reason. William H. Kooienga states:

> Our culture tends to belittle imagery: "it's just your imagination." Imagery is looked on as pictures in a story book: nice, but not necessary. This attitude assumes that imagery belongs to children, to the world of the fantastic instead of the world of the real. It is the imagery of a message, however, that helps stimulate the listener. It may be necessary for the preacher to think as a child,

and see imaginatively, to present God's truth in a moving manner. Those who listen also have a child inside who delights in an imaginative presentation. Cultural dogmas aside, images move as well as persuade people and so accomplish a major purpose in preaching.[13]

The effectiveness of demonstrations depends upon the quality and proper usage of materials selected, and the use of evocative language.

When speakers communicate a new idea in a manner that connects it to what a person already perceives, they foster understanding. Language may do that by painting a word picture. It may also make use of senses other than sight. When preachers receive the response, "Ah, now I see," they have tapped the persuasive power of evocative language."

PUBLIC SPEAKING

In developing good public address, there are a number of important factors to consider. One of the greatest assets a minister can have is the ability to articulate or to speak clearly. Proper usage of the following terms will help to make any public presentation vibrant and effective:

(1) Projection–the art of throwing the voice to speak loud enough to be heard by an entire audience.

(2) Rate–the measure of a thing by its relation to a standard. Speaking too fast makes it difficult for the listeners to understand everything being said. On the other hand, speaking too slowly can bore the audience and cause them to easily be distracted.

(3) Pronunciation–indicate the sound of a word by phonetic symbols. Seek to find the proper pronunciation of words especially unfamiliar ones.

(4) Vocal variety–a raising and lowering of the voice for emphasis and expression. Avoid speaking in a monotone. Expression is vitally important to maintain the audience's attention.

(5) Vocal distractions–this is the use of "fill-ins" while speaking, such as "uh," "er," "you know," etc. It is better to pause and gather your thoughts than to use excessive fill-ins. People may focus on the

continual use of vocal distractions and miss the meaning of the presentation itself.

(6) Eye contact–the ability to look at the person or people to whom you are speaking is developed through continuous practice. Endeavor to include everyone in the listening audience by looking from side to side. It is important to make everyone present feel that they are a significant part of the presentation.

(7) Energy–if the presenter shows excitement and interest in the subject presented the audience will become more interested.

(8) Content clarity–all material should be presented with a clear understanding, not vague or clouded in obscurity.

(9) Organization–make sure that information is in order so that it flows easily from one point to another. Use transitional words or phrases.

In addition, it is important that the voice is developed, trained, and tempered in order to be effective. The human voice is one of the most important tools in the area of communication. When used properly, it can captivate an audience and hold their attention as thoughts are expressed and skillfully delivered. The development of the voice can be done through breathing exercises, verbal exercises using the teeth, tongue, palate, and jaw and speaking aloud over emphasizing sounds, syllables, and word endings.

FOOD FOR THOUGHT

- A conscientious preacher would never attempt to deliver a message without sufficient preparation.

- The purpose of the sermon should be defined

- There must be a period of time spent in developing the ideas that God gives.

- A sermon that is God-inspired and properly developed holds great potential.

- Your thoughts must take on form before they can be effective.

- Unorganized thoughts presented in a sermon will only foster confusion.

- Each sermon should be viewed as a work of perfection.

- The minister should set the tone of the message in the early stages of preparation.

- There is a need to find out what God said and what it means.

- If the Word of God is to be interpreted correctly, it must be interpreted literally.

- The development of the sermon should be based on an understanding and practical application of the scripture text.

- The most effective preaching will consists of words about the Lord and words from the Lord.

- The text must be treated reverently and intelligently.

- The development of the ideas of a sermon always should manifest an element of creativity.

- A master of rhetoric exudes an air of eloquence.

- Style plays an important part in the delivery of a sermon.

- Demonstrations add color and excitement to sermons.

THE PRESENTATION

Regardless of how well a sermon is prepared, if it is not presented well it loses its effectiveness. After spending time gathering data, arranging the thoughts, preparing an outline, and making sure that everything is complete, the time comes when the message must be delivered. Now the rhetorical skills of the orator are put to the test. How well will the message be received? Will it achieve desired results from its listeners?

The congregation sits, waiting to be fed from the Word of God. Their souls are thirsty. There are needs to be met. Many of them are anxiously waiting to hear the voice of God speaking through his servant. The preacher rises from his seat, approaches the pulpit, and places his Bible and manuscript upon it. Now what? Will the minister rise to meet the occasion?

TRADITIONAL PREACHING

The sermon begins with a call to prayer, impressing upon the congregation to ask the Lord to uplift their hearts through the Word. The preacher then reads his text and begins his sermon. He expresses his ideas in the measured cadence of a formal style. Throughout the sermon, noted authors are quoted indicating the minister's wide range of reading. His education and intellect are revealed through the use of an extensive vocabulary. He stands erect, shoulders straight and held back, and his hands are positioned on either side of the lectern as if to secure his stance. The sermon is delivered almost word for word from his manuscript. Every word is used properly, and each sentence carries a precise meaning. The "hallelujahs" and the "amens" have been strategically placed throughout the written composition and are read along with the other data.

The delivery of the monologue is deliberate, concise, and almost devoid of emotion. Occasionally, the preacher might point his finger or slightly elevate his voice to place emphasis on a particular statement of fact. Some ministers feel that there is no place for emotion during the presentation of a religious discourse. They contend that if a person becomes emotional while preaching, the message they are trying to convey to the congregation is unrealized.

Thusly, the traditional preacher tends to concentrate on the areas of intellect, proper composition, and closely adhering to standard pulpit etiquette.

THE EXCESSES OF PREACHING

Preaching, like any other activity, can be taken to an extreme. It is the author's contention that some ministers are overly dramatic and cause the congregation to focus on the messenger instead of the message. The excessive use of theatrics in the presentation of a sermon can produce fruitless results, especially if the sermon is lacking in content.

Many times we have heard the expression "Oh, he really preached." The usual response is, "Really? What was the sermon about?" Lamentably, the congregation usually has not been given enough of the Word of God to grasp a complete thought. Therefore, their comments are geared toward the preacher's actions and not the sermon itself. "I really don't know what he preached about, but it sounded good." Here we are confronted with the act of appealing to the ear and not the heart of man.

Another type of preacher approaches the congregation with a warm smile and a pleasant demeanor. He uses a bit of humor to begin his message and proceeds to illustrate a point with a succession of stories. He continues with other thoughts loosely associated with the Scriptures. Some comments on godliness and everyday life are followed by another sequence of stories. The sermon is then concluded with a heart-rending tale.

Still another preacher enters the pulpit with a rapid-paced message ranging from the past to the future. The language used is dithyrambic and is punctuated by peaks of excitement. He walks back and forth across the platform gesturing energetically as he goes. The pulpit begins to vibrate with unveiled emotion. Although the presentation is interesting to watch, it leaves something to be desired in the area of edification.

Lastly, there is the preacher who has a lot of zeal but little knowledge. He has not taken the time to study to get a good understanding of Scripture before attempting to preach to the congregation. He lives under the misconception that all he has to do is open his mouth and the Lord will speak for him. This results in an empty, albeit emotional presentation with total sterility of the Holy Spirit's power.

THE PENTECOSTAL RESOLUTION

After previewing the sermons of a number of traditional ministers and their diversified preaching styles, we find that there seems to be something lacking in each presentation. Is it possible to extract some qualities from non-traditional ministers to have a well-prepared sermon with effective delivery?

> What would an ideal preacher sound like? How would he preach so that the message would penetrate the minds and hearts of people? Listen to one more preacher. This one has a vital message from the Scriptures to minister to the needs of his hearers. His sermon shows thoughtful organization and logical progression. In addition, he demonstrates stylistic techniques that allow his message to speak. He's clear: his word choice does not cloud the thought. He's captivating: his expressions and choice illustrations demand attention. More than that, he's penetrating: his language stirs the emotions. The pictures drawn by his word choice are powerful; his statements are phrased to linger. His conscious, thoughtful use of language propels the message to his listeners.

There is another important element present that makes this preacher's presentation most effective–the in-filling of the Holy Spirit. Man's rhetorical skills alone are not sufficient to penetrate the hearts of men and cause them to be blessed. Let us take a lesson from the Word of the Lord given to Zerubbabel, saying, "Not by might, nor by power, but by my spirit saith the Lord of hosts." (Zech. 4:6)

It is necessary for the gospel to be preached with power to bring men to salvation. Therefore, the minister must have the power of the Holy Spirit in his life. With it, he possesses the authority to bind, loose, cast out devils, heal the sick, and speak with new tongues. The same power that equipped Peter to preach on the Day of Pentecost and caused 3,000 souls to be saved is prevalent in today's well-trained Pentecostal preachers.

The difference between a Pentecostal rhetoric and a non-Pentecostal religious rhetoric becomes apparent. The power of persuasion lies in the abilities of the orator. A good speaker can possibly cause a man's mind to be changed; however, a good speaker empowered by the Holy Spirit can cause a man's life to be changed.

The Pentecostal preacher employs a combination of hermeneutics, homiletics, rhetoric, emotion, with the power of the Holy Spirit in the forefront leading him in achieving his sermon objectives. He is not limited to the basic fundamentals of preaching and is not bound by traditional pulpit etiquette. He is best described as a hybrid preacher, composed of a fundamentalist's literal interpretation of the Bible and a Pentecostal's liberty to preach under the anointing of the Holy Spirit. Shall we call him a "Fundacostal" or a "Pentemendalist"?

FOOD FOR THOUGHT

- A sermon loses its effectiveness if it is not well prepared.

- The traditional preacher usually concentrates on the areas of intellect, proper composition, and adhering to standard pulpit etiquette.

- Preaching can be taken to an extreme.

- Excessive use of theatrics in a sermon can produce fruitless results.

- Humor should be limited in biblical discourse.

- Lots of zeal with little knowledge results in an empty emotional presentation with no power.

- The Pentecostal preacher employs a combination of hermeneutics, homiletics, rhetoric, and emotion with the power of the Holy Spirit.

- A good speaker can possibly cause a man's mind to be changed; a good speaker empowered by the Holy Spirit can cause a man's life to be changed.

SUMMARY

The purpose of this study has been to identify what may be called a Pentecostal rhetoric, and to consider the impact of the Pentecostal's use of rhetorical skills. The study sought to analyze the effectiveness of traditional religious rhetoric and Pentecostal rhetoric. In making this analysis, a rationale of rhetorical criticism has been employed.

Based upon these preliminary observations, it appears that there is indeed a uniquely Pentecostal rhetoric. From what is admittedly a somewhat superficial investigation of the non-Pentecostal rhetoric, there seems to be identifiable differences. These differences can be grouped in three observable categories, namely: the degree to which the Holy Spirit's power is manifested in the presentation of the sermon, the extent to which emotion is exhibited in the preaching, and the level to which pulpit etiquette is observed.

In an attempt to ascertain the worth of a Pentecostal rhetoric, the author attempted to observe its effectiveness. It is the considered opinion of this author that the power of a Pentecostal rhetoric is superior to a non-Pentecostal religious rhetoric in its effectiveness. This can be seen in the active participation of the audience and the apparent feeling of spiritual well-being that the Pentecostal rhetoric seems to induce.

While these observations are descriptive of the macrocosmic phenomenon of the Pentecostal rhetoric, the findings of this study would seem to warrant further research into the microcosmic variables of the subject.

APPENDIX

Sermon Outlines

Will the Real Holiness Church Stand Up?

Never Saw a Man Quite Like This One

For Best Results: Follow Directions

God Will Deliver

Sermon Transcripts

Amen, Hallelujah

Re Me

After the Locusts Have Gone

The Inner Man Wants Out

We Must Go To War

What Time Is It?

Samples

Hermeneutics Worksheet

Gloria J. Lewis

Sermon Outline
12 Point Alliterative Outline
Sermon Transcript Form
Check List of Effective Study Habits

A. SERMON OUTLINES

WILL THE REAL HOLINESS CHURCH STAND UP?
I Peter 1:13–16, Hebrews 12:14, Ephesians 1:4

INTRODUCTION:

Many people, although Christians, do not want to be identified with the "holiness church." But anyone who wants to go back with Jesus when he comes will not only have to be identified with the holiness church, but will have to be a part of it.

Holiness is not merely a denomination, it is a way of life. It exemplifies purity; indicates maturity and supreme excellence; demands cleanliness, uprightness, goodness, perfectness, godliness, completeness, separation from sin, and a good conversation.

A holy walk is necessary in order to be a part of the church for which Jesus gave his life. That church is the body of believers who have been sanctified and cleansed with the washing of water by the Word. Jesus will present to himself a glorious church, not having spot or wrinkle, or any such thing; holy and without blemish (Eph. 4:27).

I. Holiness

   A. Mandated by God

       1. God created man holy and put him in a holy place where everything was good, clean and pure. Man was separated from God through sin.

       2. God commands man to be holy. (Lev. 20:7)

       3. God chose man before the foundation of the world that he should be holy. (Eph. 1:4)

   B . Mandatory for Man

       1. The state of being holy is not optional.
       2. Necessary in order to commune with God.

      a. Under the law, sacrifices were made so that man could commune with a Holy God.

      b. Sin disconnected man from God.

      c. Man expelled from the garden because of sin.

   3. Necessary in order to go back with God.

      a. Regardless of denominational affiliation.

      b. Without holiness no man shall see the Lord.

C. Manifested in Christ

   1. Perfect sacrifice—without blemish.

   2. No guile found in his mouth.

   3. In him is no sin (I John 3:5)

II. The Church (Body of Believers)

A. Purchased By God

   1. With his own blood (Acts 20:28)

   2. Gave his only begotten Son (John 3:16)

   3. I John 3:16

B. Purified By the Blood of Christ

   1. Ephesians 5:25–27.

   2. Cleanses us from all sin (I John 1:7).

3. Gave Himself for us an offering and a sacrifice to God (Eph. 5:2)

C. Preserved By the Holy Spirit

  1. I Thessalonians 5:23–24.
  2. Jude 1.

Conclusion:

The real Holiness Church is made up of believers in Jesus Christ, regardless to denomination who have patterned their lives after the plan of holiness that God has laid down for man. Now is the time to stand up and be identified with *True Holiness*.

B. NEVER SAW A MAN QUITE LIKE THIS ONE

MARK 2:1–12

INTRODUCTION:

There have been many great men whose names have gone down in history for their accomplishments, but none can be compared to the Lord Jesus Christ.

Thomas Edison discovered the electric light and made it convenient for man to see. But Jesus is the light of the world (John 8:12). Alexander Graham Bell discovered the telephone and made it possible for men to talk to each other all over the world. However, Jesus has an open communications line where he can hear all of us and talk to all of us at the same time.

I never saw a man quite like this one.

I.   The Human Side

    A. He hungered.

    B. He thirsted.

    C. He tired.

    D. He showed emotion.

II.   The Divine Side

    A. His power is realized.

        1. Saving power (Isa. 63:1)

        2. Pardoning power (Matt. 9:6, Mark 2:10)

        3. Power over nature (Luke 8:25)

        4. Life-giving power (John 17:2)

        5. Wonder-working power (Acts 10:38)

        6. Resurrection power (Rom. 1:4)

        7. Infinite power (Matt. 28:18)

    B. His power demonstrated

        1. Healed the sick.

        2. Cursed the fig tree.

3. Performed miracles.

4. Raised the dead.

CONCLUSION:

During the Lord's ministry here on earth, people realized that he was different from anyone they had ever known. He was not just a carpenter's son, prophet, or good teacher, but he was special and did things in a manner no one had ever seen before.

Today we know him as our resurrected Savior, once dead, but now alive forever more. He is our help in trouble, peace in the midst of our storms, and a bridge over troubled waters. In short, he is all of the good things wrapped up in one.

Never Saw a Man Quite Like This One!

C. FOR BEST RESULTS: FOLLOW DIRECTION

Psalms 32:8, Isaiah 55:8–9

INTRODUCTION:

If you were in need of a financial blessing and someone told you to run to the front of the room and they would completely fulfill that need, but if you walked, you would only get half of what you needed, what action would you take?

The desired outcome of an action, course, or process is achieved by adhering strictly to instructions given by one who is knowledgeable of the given situation. For every venture undertaken, one will receive some results, but not necessarily the best ones.

In our Christian walk, we must learn to use the Scriptures as our guide and walk accordingly. God told

Joshua to meditate in the book of the law both day and night so that he could observe to do all that was written therein. He was commanded not to turn from it or move to the right hand or the left. By obeying the law of God explicitly, he would become prosperous and achieve good success. We must also follow the directions given in the Word of God if we wish to prosper.

I. The Way to Walk

    A. Circumspectly (Eph. 5:15–16)

    B. In the Spirit (Gal. 5:16)

    C. Worthy (Eph.4:1)

    D. In the Light (I John 1:7)

    E. As He walked (I John 2:6)

    F. In obedience (Heb. 13:17)

II. The Way to Pray

    A. Seek the Lord continually (I Chron. 16:11)

    B. Watch and pray (Matt. 18:1)

    C. Pray always (Luke 18:1)

    D. In faith (Mark 11:24)

III. The Way to Eternal Life

    A. Renounce the world (Luke 18:28)

B. Exercise faith in Christ (John 3:14)

C. Spiritual service (John 4:35)

D. Self-sacrifice (John 12:24)

E. Obtain knowledge of God (John 17:3)

F. Sow to the Spirit (Gal. 6:8)

CONCLUSION:

If one is to achieve the highest possible results from their walk with the Lord, he must turn from his own ways, ideas and opinions, and be governed by the Word of God.

D. GOD WILL DELIVER

Daniel 3:17–18, II Cor. 1:9–10, II Tim. 4:18

INTRODUCTION:

Some years ago, when I was a teenager, my family was traveling in the mountains of West Virginia. There was snow and ice on the ground, which made driving very hazardous. My father was driving when the car hit a patch of ice and began to slide toward the edge of the mountain. When we realized the danger, my mother, my brother, and I called the name Jesus simultaneously. At that very moment the car stopped. The front wheels were almost at the edge of the cliff.

This experience was one of many, which proved to me that if you call upon the Name of the Lord, he will deliver. It doesn't matter how impossible the situation might seem, *God Will Deliver!*

I. The Hebrew Children Delivered

    A. They refused to bow down to the image the king erected.

    B. They declared God's delivering power.

    C. They were cast into the fiery furnace.

    D. The fire had no power.

II. The Apostle Paul Delivered

    A. From prison.

    B. From danger.

    C. From the sentence of death.

III. The Righteous Delivered

    A. From afflictions (Psalms 34:19)

    B. From sin and death (I Cor. 15:56–57)

    C. From temptation (I Cor. 10:13)

    D. From the midst of trouble (Psalms 91:15)

CONCLUSION:

The righteous have the blessed assurance that the Lord is always with them. Therefore, when the troubles come, He's there to deliver. He loves the Christians today as much as He loved the Hebrew children and Paul. He will do as much for us as he did for them. God is the same yesterday, today, and forever. He is a loving God, he ever cares for his own.

God Will Deliver!

E. SERMON TRANSCRIPTS

AMEN, HALLELUJAH
Psalm 106:48

Scripture Text:

Psalm 106:48–Blessed be the Lord God of
Israel from everlasting to

everlasting: and let all the people say, Amen.
Praise ye the Lord.

INTRODUCTION:

Among all the books of antiquity, none has made such
a powerful appeal to the human heart as the Psalms. In

no other book of the Bible can one find such varieties of religious experience.

The term "Psalms" comes from the LXX or the Septuagint (the Greek translation of the OT), which applies the title Psalmoi to the collection. The Codex Alexandrinus, which is one of the major Biblical manuscripts, furnishes the designation "Psalter" by using the Greek word "Psalterion." However, the Hebrew Bible uses the designation "Te hillim," which means, "Praises." We find that in rabbinical literature this same idea was carried over in the term Seper Te hillim meaning "Book of Praises." So we see then that an entire book of the Bible has been set aside for the express purpose of praising God.

MAJOR THOUGHTS:

As the Psalms were not written by one man, so neither do they form one book. The Psalter is in fact a Pentateuch, and the lines of demarcation, which divide the five books one from another, are clear and distinct. At the end of each book which is marked by Psalms 41, 72, 89, and 106, we meet with the solemn, Amen, singled or redoubled, following on a doxology which indicates that one book ends and another is about to begin.

Note that in each doxology there are always two things present … agreement and praise. The agreement is seen by the use of the word "amen," and praise is shown by "blessed be the Lord and praise ye the Lord or hallelujah." Hallelujah means praise ye Jah—a common form of adoration and thanksgiving. It is used at the beginning and close of many psalms.

Amen—so be it; may it become true—is said after a prayer, a wish, or a statement with which one agrees; used to express solemn ratification (as an expression of faith) or hearty approval. A word used to affirm and confirm a statement.

Used at the beginning of a sentence, it emphasizes what is about to be said. It is frequently so employed by our Lord and is translated "truly." It is often used to confirm the words of another and adds the wish for success to another's vows and predictions. It was a custom, which passed over from the synagogue to the Christian assemblies, that when he who had read or discoursed (preached) had offered up a solemn prayer to God the others in attendance responded "Amen," and this made the substance of what was uttered their own. Several of the church fathers refer to this custom, and Jerome says that at the conclusion of public prayer the united voice of the people sounded like the fall of water or the noise of thunder.

The people were saying in effect—I believe that it will come true, it receives my hearty approval, so blessed be the Lord and all praises go to him, so I give him the highest praise (hallelujah). I say amen and hallelujah to wonders, deliverance, spiritual victories, to knowledge and power, to divine council, for provisions, to prosperity, to health, to satisfaction of soul desires, to answered prayers, for a hearing ear, to strength and guidance and renewed faith. I say amen and hallelujah because I believe in whatever you said. So be it, it is so, I approve, I know that's right, so you're worthy of the highest praise. Hallelujah!

He said I'm with you.

I say amen, hallelujah.

He said I heard your prayer.

I say amen, hallelujah.

He said trust me I'll bring it to pass.

I say amen, hallelujah.

He said I've given you power, use it.

I say amen, hallelujah.

He said I've given you the anointing, which breaks every yoke and loose you from bondage, brings understanding, drives the enemy away, gives you courage and fulfills every longing.

I say amen, hallelujah.

He said go and I'll go with you.

I say amen, hallelujah.

He said fear not, for I am your God.

I say amen, hallelujah.

He said don't worry about tomorrow for I will provide.

I say amen, hallelujah.

He said be strong and of good courage while going through trials.

I say amen, hallelujah.

He said weeping may endure for a night, but joy comes in the morning.

I say amen, hallelujah.

He said despise not small beginnings.

I say amen hallelujah.

He said trust me in the dark.

I say amen, hallelujah.

He said I allow these things to come because you needed to be broken.

I say amen, hallelujah.

He said the troubles are working for your good.

I say amen, hallelujah.

He said I have great blessings in store for
you.

I say amen, hallelujah.

CONCLUSION:

Everything that God allows to come into our lives
is working for our good, therefore, we must learn to
acquiesce to his will, stand in agreement with him, and
give him praise.

Amen–I agree, Hallelujah–I give you the highest praise!

F. RE ME

Romans 12:1–2

I urge you, brothers, in view of God's mercy,
to offer your bodies as living sacrifices, holy
and pleasing to God—which is your spiritual worship. Do not conform any longer to
the pattern of this world, but be transformed
by the renewing of your mind. Then you
will be able to test and approve what God's
will is—his good, pleasing and perfect will.

Romans 12:1–2 (NIV)

Your mind matters in changed behavior. The Christian
finds new power to do the things he should and new
strength to resist evil. This strength for righteousness

comes through the avenue of the intellect. The key to clean living is clear thinking. What we think is manifested in our lives. It is necessary to program our minds toward those things, which are pleasing in God's sight.

There comes a time for a renewal. We need to say to the Lord: renew my mind, renew my faith, renew my worship, renew my dedication, renew me in your Spirit so that I can know your perfect will, walk in your way continually, be fruitful in my work for you.

Re—used in the formation of compound words usually to signify back or again.

Let's take a look at some "re" words:

> *Renew*–implies so extensive a remaking that what had become faded or disintegrated now seems like new.

> *Restore*–implies a return to an original state after depletion or loss.

> *Refresh*–implies the supplying of something necessary to restore lost strength, animation, or power.

> *Renovate*–suggests a renewing by cleansing, repairing, or rebuilding.

Rejuvenate–suggests the restoration of youthful vigor, powers, and appearance.

Sometimes circumstances in our lives will cause us to lose ground in our spiritual walk. It becomes necessary for us to ask as David did in Psalm 51:10 when he cried, "Create in me a clean heart O God and renew a right spirit within me."

Re–accept me
Re–acquaint me
Re–activate me
Re–appoint me
Re–approve me
Re–arouse me
Re–arrange me
Re–assign me
Re–awaken me
Re–baptize me (in your spirit)
Re–commission me
Re–connect me
Re–dedicate me
Re–endow me
Re- tune me
Re–unite me
Re–store me

Re–equip me
Re–establish me
Re–fix me
Re–fortify me
Re–vigorate me
Re–motivate me
Re–accentuate me
Re–adorn me
Re–accessorize me
Re–anoint me
Re–purify me
Re–strengthen me
Re–teach me
Re–transform me
Re–utilize me
Re–wash me
Re–make me

Re–mold me   Re–use me

So that I can:

> Rejoice in you
>
> Reflect your light
>
> Reassure others
>
> Rebuild broken fellowships
>
> Receive your blessings
>
> Reduce in self
>
> Reaffirm your Word
>
> Refuse to give in or up
>
> Regain my place in you
>
> Remember who you are
>
> Repel all unrighteousness

Re Me! I need you, Lord, to take me and make me all over again. I want to be what you want me to be. Not my will but thine be done. My mind, my body, and my soul belong to you. I am no longer my own. You have bought me with a great price, the shedding of your precious blood. I now belong to you and you can do with me as you please.

I recognize that I have not always done things right.

I have not crossed every "t" or dotted every "i." I have come short in many areas of my life and I need a renewing. *Re Me Lord!*

G. AFTER THE LOCUST HAVE GONE

Joel 2:19–27

SCRIPTURE TEXT:

Yea, the Lord will answer and say unto his people, Behold, I will send you corn, and wine, and oil, and ye shall be satisfied therewith: and I will no more make you a reproach among the heathen: But I will remove far off from you the northern army, and will drive him into a land barren and desolate, with his face toward the east sea, and his hinder part toward the utmost sea, and his stink shall come up, and his ill savour shall come up, because he hath done great things. Fear not, O land; be glad and rejoice: for the Lord will do great things. Be not afraid, ye beasts of the field: for the pastures of the wilderness do spring, for the tree beareth her fruit, the fig tree and the vine do yield their strength. Be glad then, ye children of Zion, and rejoice in the Lord your God: for he hath given you the former rain moderately, and he will cause to come down for you the rain, the former rain, and the latter rain in the first month. And the floors shall be full of wheat; and the fats shall overflow with wine and oil. And I will restore to you the years that the locust hath eaten, the cankerworm, and the caterpillar, and the palmerworm, my great army which I sent among you. And ye shall eat in plenty, and be satisfied, and praise the name of the Lord your God, that hath dealt wondrously with you and my people shall never be ashamed. And ye shall know that I am in the midst of Israel, and that I am the Lord your God, and none else; and my people shall never be ashamed.

Joel 2:19–27

INTRODUCTION:

What happens when the locusts come? Destruction takes place; pain and a sense of loss sets in; dark clouds hover over our dreams, aspirations, and accomplishments; day turns to night; we are left empty and desolate, discouraged, betrayed, and heartbroken; it brings doubt that there is a way to rebuild, or that there's anything left to plant. It's during these times that we must be assured that when calamity comes it brings the opportunity to trust and depend on God, partner with him and be restored to wholeness.

Thus bringing us to another searching question:

What happens after the locusts have gone?

MAJOR THOUGHTS:

Locusts belong to the class of Orthoptera, i.e. straight-winged. They are of many species. The ordinary Syrian locust resembles the grasshopper, but is larger and more destructive. "The legs and thighs of these insects are so powerful that they can leap to a height of two hundred times the length of their bodies. When so raised they spread their wings and fly so close together as to appear like one compact moving mass."

The devastation they make in Eastern lands is often very appalling. The invasions of locusts are the heaviest calamities that can befall a country. "Their numbers exceed computation: the Hebrews called them "the countless," and the Arabs knew them as 'the darkeners of the sun.' Unable to guide their own flight, though capable of crossing large spaces, they are at the mercy of the wind, which bears them as blind instruments of Providence to the doomed region given over to them for the time. Innumerable as the drops of water or the sands of the seashore, their flight obscures the sun and casts a thick shadow on the earth. It seems indeed as if a great aerial mountain, many miles in breadth, were advancing with a slow, unresting progress. Woe to the countries beneath them if the wind fall and let them alight! They descend unnumbered as flakes of snow and hide the ground. It may be 'like the garden of Eden before them, but behind them is a desolate wilderness. At their approach, the people are in anguish. No walls can stop them; no ditches arrest them; fires kindled in their path are forthwith extinguished by the myriad of their dead, and the countless armies march on. If a door or a window were open, they enter and destroy every-thing of wood in the house. Every terrace, court, and inner chamber is filled with them in a moment. Such an awful visitation swept over Egypt (Exodus10:1–19), consuming before it every green thing and stripping the trees, until the land was bared of all signs of vegetation. A strong north-west wind from the Mediterranean swept the locusts into the Red Sea.

Locusts can invade in many forms: a failed marriage, death of a loved one, abuse, financial ruin, family problems, addictions, sickness, and sometimes the consequences of our own foolish actions.

We must be assured that the heavens once again will be opened, the drought will end, the locusts will disappear, the harvest will return, and the Lord's presence will be realized.

God wanted to bring restoration and healing to His people. True repentance was needed—certain fruit will demonstrate a true repentance (fasting, weeping, and mourning).

—Fast now so that you may be filled later

—Mourn now so that you can be comforted later.

Three assurances are given:

1. To the land—where it was completely devastated it will be completely restored.

2. To the beasts of the field—God will restore all vegetation so they will have ample food to eat.

3. To the children of Zion—God makes five specific promises:

    a. He will provide rain for crops

    b. He will provide abundant harvests of grain and grapes

c. Make up for the devastation suffered by the locust plague

d. Provide abundant food and end the famine

e. Most of all, he will cause his people to know that he is Jehovah their God and there is no other God than he.

Joel never tried to explain *why* disaster arrived. There's not much comfort in asking *why*. When we dwell on the why, it brings about more pain, more confusion, and more discouragement. But if we begin to examine the *how*, that's when healing begins. When we find the courage to acquiesce to the will of God and work alongside Him, the barren fields will produce again.

God's plan for restoration in the Book of Joel.

First–spend the night in sackcloth (1:13) and be authentic in our sorrow, for this marks the turning point.

Second–then comes emotional spring cleaning as we "declare a holy fast" (1:14), letting go of any bitterness, anger at God, any attitude or behavior lurking about ready to sabotage our lives.

Third–"Return to the Lord your God with all your heart"

CONCLUSION:

What began in disappointment and darkness will end in joy and spiritual plenty. Hold on to your dreams, aspirations or goals because after the dry season comes the harvest. After the locusts have gone, the reproduction process begins and the latter shall be greater than the former.

H. THE INNER MAN WANTS OUT

John 12:24–25, Mark 14:3–6

Verily, verily, I say unto you, Except a corn of wheat fall into the ground and die, it abideth alone: but if it die, it bringeth forth much fruit. He that loveth his life shall lose it; and he that hateth his life in this world shall keep it unto life eternal.

John 12:24–25

And being in Bethany in the house of Simon the leper, as he sat at meat, there came a woman having an alabaster box of ointment of spikenard very precious; and she brake the box, and poured it on his head.

Mark 14: 3–6

INTRODUCTION:

Man is a triune being made up of body, soul, and spirit. The body being the outermost man, the soul the outer man and the spirit the inner man. God intended for man's spirit to be his home or dwelling place. So the Holy Spirit making union with the human spirit was to govern the soul, and the spirit and soul would use the body as the means of expression.

MAJOR THOUGHTS:

The soul, instead of functioning individually, must become the organ or vessel for the spirit. So it is the independent action of the soul that must be destroyed. Our whole human nature is in our souls, and if nature is suppressed in one direction, she will take revenge in another. As an instrument, the soul has to be won, mastered, and ruled in relation to the higher and different ways of God. It is spoken of so frequently in the Scriptures as being some thing over which we have to gain and exercise authority:

> Luke 21:19–In your patience possess ye your souls.

> I Peter 1:22–ye have purified your souls in obedience to the truth.

> I Peter 1:9–The end of your faith, even the salvation of your souls.

So we see why the soul (outer man) must be broken, mastered, and renewed for the spirit to use. Anyone who serves God will discover sooner or later that the great hindrance to his work is not others but himself. His outward man and his inward man are not in harmony. He will also sense the inability of his outward man to submit to the spirit's control, thus rendering him incapable of obeying God's commands. The greatest difficulty lies in his outward man, because it hinders him from using his spirit. The Bible divides man into two parts:

> Romans 7:22 says, "For I delight in the law of God according to the inward man," Our inward man delights in the Law of God.

> Ephesians 3:16 says, " … To be strengthened with power by his Spirit in the inner man." And Paul tells us in II Corinthians 4:16, "But though our outward man perish, yet the inward man is renewed day by day." When God comes to indwell us by his

> Spirit, life, and power, he comes into our
> spirit, which is the inward man.

Outside of this inward man is the soul wherein function our thoughts, emotions and will. The outermost man is our physical body. Our inward man is the human spirit where God dwells, where His Spirit mingles with our spirit. Just as we are dressed in clothes, so our inward man "wears" an outward man: the spirit "wears" the soul. And similarly, the spirit and soul "wear" the body. We must recognize that he who can work for God is the one whose inward man can be released. The basic difficulty of a servant of God lies in the failure of the inward man to break through the outward man. The Lord wants to break our outward man in order that the inward man may have a way out. When the inward man is released, both unbelievers and believers will be blessed. Nature has its way of breaking. The Lord tells us in John 12, "Except the grain of wheat falls into the ground and dies, it abides alone; but if it die, it bears much fruit." Life is in the grain of wheat, but there is a shell, a very hard shell on the outside. As long as that shell is not split open, the wheat cannot sprout and grow. The dying is the cracking open of the shell through the working together of temperature and humidity in the soil. Once the shell is split open, the wheat begins to grow. So the question here is not whether there is life within, but whether the outside shell is cracked open. The Scripture continues by saying, "He that loves his life (Greek, soul) shall lose it, and he that hates his life (Greek, soul) in this world shall keep it to life eternal." The Lord shows us here that the outer shell is our own life (our soul life), while the life within is the eternal life which he has given to us. To allow the inner life to come forth it is imperative that the outward life be replaced. Should the outward remain unbroken, the inward would never be able to come forth. If the alabaster box is not broken, the pure spikenard will not flow forth. Strange to say, many are still treasuring the alabaster box, thinking that its value exceeds that of the ointment. Many think that their outward man is more precious than their inward man. This becomes the problem in the church. One will treasure his cleverness, thinking he is quite important; another will treasure his own emotions, esteeming himself as an important person; others highly regard themselves, feeling they are better than others, their eloquence surpasses that of others, they feel superior. However, we are not vase admirers, or ancient artifact collectors, but we are those who desire to smell only the sweet smell of the balm. Without the breaking of the outward, the inward will not come forth. With the outward man unbroken, an intelligent person's mind governs his work; if he is a tenderhearted person, his sensitivity controls his actions. Such work may appear prosperous but cannot bring people to God. Secondly, his spirit may come forth clothed in his own thoughts or emotions. We must realize that it is the Spirit, which quickens. When the outward man is completely broken—there will be an end to outward movement with inward numbness—an end to inward crying with outward calmness—an end to an overflow of inner thoughts for which there is no pronouncement. We will abide increasingly in God—our spirit can receive divine illumination—we may most inadvertently contact the spirit in others by our spirit—whenever one speaks in our presence, we can "size him up"—evaluate what kind of person he is, what attitude he is taking, or what his need is. Our spirit can touch his spirit—with some, we only meet their thoughts, their emotions, or their will. The outer shell is too thick for others to touch the inner man.

CONCLUSION:

With the breaking of the outward man, the spirit begins to flow and is ever open to others. Once the outward man is broken man's spirit very naturally abides in the presence of God without ceasing. Our response to outward things change. God does not deliver us from the noise that's going on around us but he delivers us from our responses.

When the outward man is broken, outside things will be kept outside, and the inward man will live before

God continuously. The outward man is broken through the disciple of the Holy Spirit! The breaking of the outward man must be accomplished before God can use us in an effective manner.

I. WE MUST GO TO WAR

SCRIPTURE TEXT:

And unto Adam he said, because thou hast
hearkened unto the voice of thy wife, and
hast eaten of the tree, of which I commanded thee, saying, Thou shalt not eat of
it: cursed is the ground for thy sake; in sorrow shalt thou eat of it all the days of thy
life; Thorns also and thistles shall it bring
forth to thee; and thou shalt eat the herb of
the field; In the sweat of thy face shalt thou
eat bread, till thou return unto the ground;
for out of it wast thou taken: for dust

thou art, and into dust shalt thou return.

Genesis 3:17–19

(For the weapons of our warfare are not carnal, but mighty through God to the pulling down of strong holds;) Casting down imaginations, and every high thing that exalteth itself against the knowledge of God, and bringing into captivity every thought to the obedience of Christ; And having in a readiness to revenge all disobedience, when your obedience is fulfilled.

II Corinthians 10:4–6

INTRODUCTION:

When sin entered the world, it brought about some devastating changes. It was purposed in the mind of God when he created man that man would live forever in a glorious state. However, when man sinned, things began to fall apart. He died spiritually, the death process began in the physical body, and the earth changed and the ground stopped yielding freely.

A dark shadow was cast upon the earth because of sin. Man no longer enjoyed the glorious light of God, but he began to walk in darkness. Every since the expulsion from the garden, man has had downward tendencies. He's traveled downward into valleys of sorrow, despair, and depravity. He looks down and falls down. When he would do good, evil is always present, and because of the downward tendencies, man finds it difficult to do the things he wants to do.

MAJOR THOUGHTS:

Before sin there were no:

- thorns or thistles
- sickness or diseases
- troubled waters
- deserts
- unfertile ground
- reasons to till the ground
- tears
- pain
- turmoil
- wrath
- heresies
- drunkenness
- distress
- sorrow
- sadness
- grief
- sleepless nights
- worrying
- depression
- bad habits
- addictions
- strife
- envyings
- revellings
- adultery
- fornication
- uncleanness
- lasciviousness
- idolatry
- witchcraft
- hatred
- variance
- emulations
- seditions
- murders

Sin has caused devastation in our lives. The devil has stolen many things from us. Sin is destroying the lives of our loved ones and tearing down the family unit. It's causing havoc in the church and bringing divisions.

So I have come to the conclusion that we as Saints of God must declare war on sin and Satan. We must get dressed for spiritual warfare and stand until the battle is won. Must means obliged or required to; compelled to; no conscientious objectors, and no draft dodgers. We must realize that the weapons of our warfare are not carnal, but spiritual. There are strongholds that must come down and are only conquered through the spirit. The Apostle Paul writing to the church at Corinth admonished them to put on spiritual armor, and use spiritual weapons in spiritual warfare to gain spiritual victory.

I have found out that the best defense is a good offense. We have been sitting back and allowing the enemy to attack us. It is time to turn the tables and attack the enemy. We can attack him with the assurance that we are the victors. We have the power to go over into the enemy's camp and take back everything he has stolen from us. Get fighting mad and take back your homes, your finances, your peace of mind, your children, your joy, your happiness, your healing, your deliverance, your self-esteem, your dignity and everything that is rightfully yours. In addition, we must cast down evil imagination, self-exaltation, spiritual pride, stand in readiness to enforce church discipline and revenge all disobedience. It is necessary to get totally prepared for war.

"Finally, my brethren, be strong in the Lord, and in the power of his might. Put on the whole armour of God, that ye may be able to stand against the wiles of the devil. For we wrestle not against flesh and blood, but against principalities, against powers, against the rulers of the darkness of this world, against spiritual wickedness in high places. Wherefore take unto you the whole armour of God, that ye may be able to withstand in the evil day, and having done all, to stand. Stand therefore, having your loins girt about with truth, and having on the breastplate of righteousness; And your feet shod with the preparation of the gospel of peace; Above all, taking the shield of faith, wherewith ye shall be able to quench all the fiery darts of the wicked. And take the helmet of salvation, and the sword of the Spirit, which is the word of God: Praying always with all prayer and supplication in the Spirit, and watching thereunto with all perseverance and supplication, for all saints."

Ephesians 6:10–18

CONCLUSION:

A songwriter wrote,

> Am I a soldier of the cross, follower of the Lamb? Should I fear to own his cause or blush to speak his Name? Must I be carried to the sky on flowery beds of ease, while others fought to win the prize, and sailed on bloody seas? Sure I must fight if I would reign; increase my courage, Lord. I'll bear the toil, endure the pain, supported by thy Word.[14]

There is no other recourse: We Must Go to War!

J. WHAT TIME IS IT?

II Timothy 3:1–7

INTRODUCTION:

Time plays a very important role in all of our lives. People are constantly asking, "What time is it?" Down through the years men have used many methods and means to tell time. Some could look at the sun, its position, how the shadows were cast and tell the time. Then there was the use of sundials and the clock came along.

There are clocks with pendulums, and clocks with minute and second hands, electric clocks, and battery operated clocks. In addition, there are watches of all kinds. There are not only wristwatches, but watches you can hang around your neck, pin on your clothes, wear on your fingers, and display on cellular phones.

With all of these means and methods of telling time, there are still so many people who still don't know what time it is. If the question, "What time is it?" was asked of someone, no doubt their first reaction would be to look at their watch or at a clock. But today as I ask this question of you, I don't want you to look at your watch or a clock. Instead, I implore you to look in the Word of God, then take a good look around you, and tell me what time it is.

MAJOR POINTS

In these verses of scripture, we find symptoms of "final days" disease:

- Lovers of their own selves—selfish
- Covetous—desiring things that belong to others.
- Boasters—speaking too highly of oneself or what one owns.
- Proud—thinking too well of oneself; haughty; arrogant.
- Blasphemous—speaks about God or sacred things with abuse or contempt.
- Disobedient to parents—refusing to obey
- Unthankful—ungrateful, not appreciative, thankless.

- Unholy–wicked, sinful
- Without natural affection–not loving in the manner that God purposed for man.
- Trucebreakers–breaking the peace, start fighting again
- False accusers–liars
- Incontinent–lack of self-control, an inability to restrain sexual indulgences.
- Fierce–savage
- Despisers of those that are good
- Traitors–reckless
- High-minded–drunk with pride
- Lovers of pleasure more than lovers of God
- Having a form of godliness but denying the power thereof–having religion without the redeemer
- Ever learning and never able to come to the knowledge of the truth–hold information without illumination.

Men assume the form of godliness to take away their reproach, but they will not submit to the power of it to take away their sin. They can have the form and be totally destitute of the power.

We see that all of these things are present in today's society. We see it in the newspapers, on the television, on worldwide news, in our neighborhoods, and in our homes. Yet many of us still don't know or refuse to see what time it is. Surely, we are living in perilous times. We may very well be the generation that will not see death, but will be caught up to meet the Lord in the air.

What time is it?

It's time to watch

It's time to work

It's time to live holy

Its time to put away all foolishness

It's time to stop playing church

It's time to really know that you are saved

It's time to let the devil know that he has no place in you and no power over you

It's time to put on the whole armor of God so that you will be able to fight against the wiles of the devil

It's time to wake up

It' time to get up

It's time to dress up

It's time to confess up

It's time to keep up

It's time to stay up

It's time to put away the idol gods

If the church really wants to know what time it is:

It's time to walk in power

It's time to heal the sick

It's time to loose the bound

It's time to set the prisoners free

It's time to bring deliverance to the drug addicts, the alcoholics, and the prostitutes

It's time to close down the crack houses

It's time to lift up a standard of holiness

It's time to serve Satan notice that his kingdom is coming down

It's time to triumph over the enemy

CONCLUSION:

If you really want to know what time it is, it's almost midnight and the Lord is on his way back. And when he shall come and gather up his own, time will be no more. We are going to step out of time over into eternity to forever be with the Lord. Therefore, it's time to get ready to meet your God.

K. HERMENEUTICS WORKSHEET

SCRIPTURE TEXT:
Historical Background

Cultural Background

Occasion of the Writing

Parallel Scriptures

Interpretation

Exegesis

Application

Source of References

Commentaries Used

Other References

Personal Experiences

L. SERMON OUTLINE

The Introduction –(Tells them what you are going to tell them)

    -Use Startling opening statement (Gets the attention of the congregation)

       Can be a quotation, question, etc.

The Body – (Tells them)

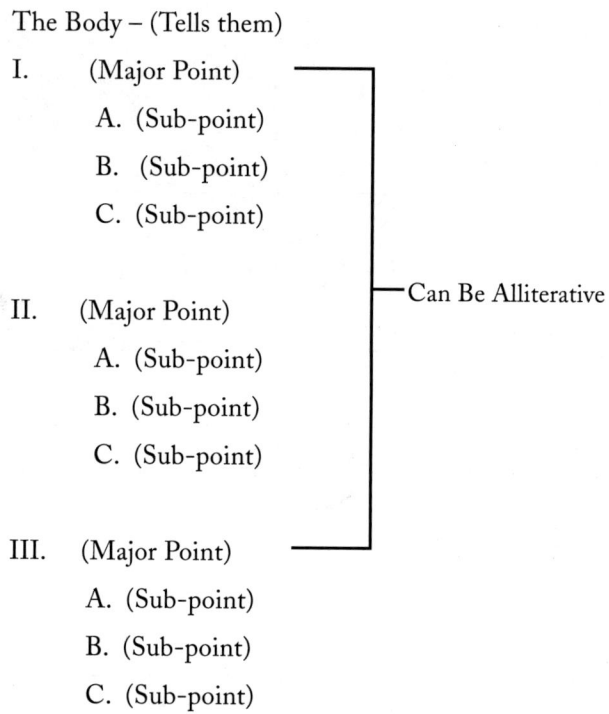

I.   (Major Point)

     A. (Sub-point)

     B. (Sub-point)

     C. (Sub-point)

II.   (Major Point)

     A. (Sub-point)

     B. (Sub-point)

     C. (Sub-point)

Can Be Alliterative

III.   (Major Point)

     A. (Sub-point)

     B. (Sub-point)

     C. (Sub-point)

Conclusion – (Tells them what you told them)
   -Closing Statement (should be thought provoking)
  Note: Sub-points may also be alliterative.

M. 12 POINT
ALLITERATIVE OUTLINE

Introduction

Body

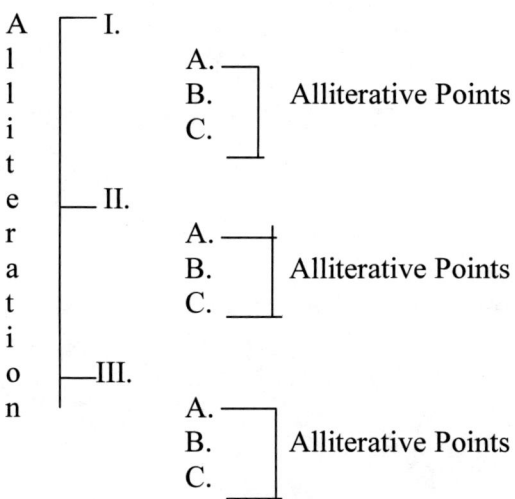

Conclusion

N.   SERMON PLAN FORM

Theme	Subject of Discourse
	Purpose of Discourse
Songs	Introduction…
Scriptures	
(any further expressions)	Main Points…
	Conclusion
Comments	
Continuation Sheet	

O.   CHECK LIST OF EFFECTIVE STUDY HABITS

How many of the following questions can you answer with a "yes"?

_____1. As a rule, do you get eight hours sleep per night?

_____2. Do you have the necessary study material, tools, and equipment for proper study?

_____3. Do you read reasonably fast, always seeking the main ideas?

_____4. Do you look up the definitions of new words?

_____5. Do you stop at the end of a passage or a chapter to review in your own words that which you have just studied?

_____6. Do you have a specific time for study each day?

_____7. Do you have a definite place for study?

_____8. Is your study place conducive to productivity?

_____9. When studying over a long period, do you take an occasional break?

_____10. Do you prevent yourself from being distracted by daydreaming while you are studying?

_____11. Do you prepare an outline?

_____12. Are your outlines such that they are beneficial to you for review at a later time?

_____13. Are all points in your outline taken from the text?

_____14. Do you refer to comparative bible passages or other related material?

_____15. Do you make notes concerning wider implications?

_____16. Do you use the basic principles of hermeneutics in interpreting text?

_____17. Are distractions at a minimum during your study time?

_____18. Are you enthusiastic about the material studied?

_____19. Do you read the text at least five times?

_____20. Do you study with an attitude of prayer?

_____21. Do you study with an open mind?

_____22. Do you identify yourself with the speaker?

_____23. Do you use your imagination (without getting carried away) as you read the text?

_____24. Do you express concisely the main points of the text?

_____25. Do you note what is questionable in the passage of scripture?

_____26. Do you compare different translations to see if there is any notable disagreement?

_____27. Do you identify key words or theories found in the text?

_____28. Do you list historical, literary or theological issues apparent in the text?

_____29. Do you study even when you are not scheduled to make a presentation?

Score yourself on "yes" answers as follows:

27 or higher   Excellent
You are on the road to success.

23-26   Good

You have most of the study habits required for success and
can easily develop the few study skills you have missed.

18-22   Fair

You possess some good study habits but must
develop a few more to put you on the right road.

ENDNOTES

Chapter 1

1   Weirsbe, Warren, *Listen! Jesus is Praying* (Tyndale Second Printing Living Studies Edition, March 1983) p. 144

2   Heflin, Wallace H., *The Power of prophecy* (McDougal Publishing, 1006)

Chapter 2

3   Unger, Merrill F., *Principles of Expository Preaching* (Grand Rapids, Zondervan 1955), p. 18

4 Wilder, Amos, *Theopoetic Theology and the Religious Imagination (Philadelphia Fortress, (1976)*

5 Craddock, Fred B., *Preaching* (June 1990), p. 177
Chapter 3

6 Vines, Jerry, *A Practical Guide to Sermon Preparation*, p.3

7 Best, Ernest, *From Text to Sermon: Responsible Use of the New Testament in Preaching* (Atlanta, John Knox, 1978), pp. 97–99

8 Johnson, Joseph, *Proclamation Theology*, (Shreveport, La: Fourth Episcopal District Press, 1977), pp. 46–47

9 Virkler, Henry A., *Hermeneutics Principles and Processes of Biblical Interpretation*, pp. 45–46

Chapter 4

10 Blackwood, Andrew, *The Preparation of Sermons*, (Nashville, Abingdon, 1948), p. 18

11 Thomssen, Baird, Braden, *Speech Criticism*,

(New York: The Ronald Press Company, 1948)

12   Koonienga, William H., *Elements of Style for Preaching* (Grand Rapids: Zondervan, 1989)

13   Buttrick, David, *Homiletics Moves and Structures* (Fortress Press, 1987) pp. 199–200

Appendix

14   "Am I a Soldier?" Words: Watts, Isaac, 1674–1748, Music: Arlington, Arne, Thomas A. arr. by Harrison, Ralph (McNally, McIntosh, Rigdon M.)

BIBLIOGRAPHY

Felder, Cain Hope, *Stony the Road We Trod*: (Minneapolis: Fortress Press, 1991)

McDowell, Josh. *Syllabus on Communication and Persuasion.* ([Missing publishing information.]1983).

McQuilkin, Robertson. *Understanding and Applying The Bible:* (Chicago: Moody Press, 1983, 1992).

Pattison, T. Harwood. *The Making of the Sermon*: (Valley Forge: Judson Press, 1979).

Thonssen, Lester, Baird, A. Craig, and Braden, Waldo W. *Speech Criticism.* 2nd ed.: (New York: The Ronald Press Company, 1970).

Wichelins, H. A. "The Literary Criticism of Oratory," *Studies in Rhetoric and Public Speaking in Honor of J. A. Winans:* (New York: The Century Company, 1925).

listen|imagine|view|experience

AUDIO BOOK DOWNLOAD INCLUDED WITH THIS BOOK!

In your hands you hold a complete digital entertainment package. Besides purchasing the paper version of this book, this book includes a free download of the audio version of this book. Simply use the code listed below when visiting our website. Once downloaded to your computer, you can listen to the book through your computer's speakers, burn it to an audio CD or save the file to your portable music device (such as Apple's popular iPod) and listen on the go!

How to get your free audio book digital download:

1. Visit www.tatepublishing.com and click on the e|LIVE logo on the home page.
2. Enter the following coupon code:
   e05f-45e9-5f40-2edb-586c-c6bf-8628-63d5
3. Download the audio book from your e|LIVE digital locker and begin enjoying your new digital entertainment package today!